Community Building for Marketers

How to connect, engage
and foster growth

Areej AbuAli

First published in Great Britain and the United States in 2025 by Kogan Page Limited

Kogan Page
Kogan Page Ltd, 2nd Floor, 45 Gee Street, London EC1V 3RS, United Kingdom
Kogan Page Inc, 8 W 38th Street, Suite 90, New York, NY 10018, USA
www.koganpage.com

EU Representative (GPSR)
Authorised Rep Compliance Ltd, Ground Floor, 71 Lower Baggot Street, Dublin, D02 P593, Ireland
www.arccompliance.com

Kogan Page books are printed on paper from sustainable forests.

© Areej AbuAli, 2025

The moral rights of the author have been asserted.

ISBNs
Hardback   978 1 3986 1696 7
Paperback   978 1 3986 1693 6
Ebook   978 1 3986 1695 0

British Library Cataloguing-in-Publication Data
A CIP record for this book is available from the British Library.

Library of Congress Control Number
2024052986

Typeset by Integra Software Services, Pondicherry
Print production managed by Jellyfish
Printed and bound by CPI Group (UK) Ltd, Croydon CR0 4YY

PRAISE FOR *COMMUNITY BUILDING FOR MARKETERS*

'A gift to anyone who believes in the power of community and is ready to take the steps to build one that truly matters.'
Richard Millington, Founder, FeverBee

'It takes a special person to build communities that thrive and last. Areej AbuAli's work to create and nurture the Women in Tech SEO community is a shining example of what it looks like when heart meets execution. I'm thrilled to see her share her insights and learnings on community, as we as humans need it now more than ever. A must-read for anyone who wants to foster connection.'
Christina Garnett, Founder, Pocket CCO

'A masterclass in community building. With clear, practical guidance, tangible real-world examples, and a structured, strategic approach, this is the ultimate guide to developing a meaningful and truly impactful community, from someone who has proven themselves to be a trailblazing expert in authentic connection.'
Allegra Chapman, Co-Creator, Watch This Sp_ce

To my two Aminas, I hope I make you both proud

CONTENTS

PART FOUR Stories from community-first brands

FOREWORD

By Richard Millington

*Richard Millington is the founder of FeverBee, a community consul-
tancy, and author of* Build Your Community. *Over the past 15 years,
Richard has helped over 300 organizations, including Apple,
Facebook, Microsoft, Google, The World Bank and SAP, to use powerful psychology to build thriving communities. Through his community management academy, he has also trained 1,250 of the world's
top community pros.*

I first encountered Areej's work through her remarkable community,
Women in Tech SEO (WTS). What struck me immediately was not
just the scale of the community she had built but the authenticity and
warmth that defined it. In a world where online spaces can often feel
impersonal, WTS stood out as a vibrant, supportive network where
members truly felt seen and heard. As I got to know Areej and her
story, it became clear that this was not just the result of good fortune
or happenstance, but of deliberate, thoughtful effort rooted in a deep
understanding of what makes a community thrive.

Areej's journey, which she so candidly shares in the introduction to
this book, is one that many of us can relate to. It's a story of a passion
project born out of a personal need – one that blossomed into something far greater than she could have imagined. What began as a
small, self-created space where she could ask questions and share
experiences without fear of judgement has grown into a global community with over 10,000 members. This is a remarkable achieve-
ment, but even more impressive is how Areej has maintained the
heart and soul of that community as it has scaled.

What makes *Community Building for Marketers* such an essential
read is Areej's ability to distil her experiences into practical, actionable
advice. She doesn't just tell you what to do – she shows you how to do
it, step by step. From defining your community's purpose and culture
to navigating the challenges of growth and scale, this book is a comprehensive guide for anyone looking to build a meaningful community.

But this book is more than just a guide; it's a conversation with someone who has walked the path before you. Areej writes with a warmth and accessibility that makes you feel like you're sitting down with a trusted friend who's ready to share everything she's learned. Her insights are not just theoretical; they are grounded in real-world experience and enriched by the stories of other community-first brands she has studied and interviewed.

As someone who has spent much of my career thinking about how to create and nurture communities, I can tell you that what Areej offers here is invaluable. The world is full of online spaces – some successful, many not – but the ones that truly make a difference are those built with intention, care and a deep respect for the people who make up their membership. This book is a masterclass in how to do just that.

Whether you're just starting out or looking to breathe new life into an existing community, you'll find this book full of wisdom and practical advice that you can apply immediately. Areej has created a roadmap for success, but she's also left room for you to make it your own. The principles she lays out are adaptable to any context, allowing you to build a community that reflects your unique vision and values.

I am excited for you to dive into this book and begin your journey. There is so much potential in the communities we create, and with Areej's guidance, I have no doubt that you'll be able to unlock that potential in ways you never thought possible. This book is a gift to anyone who believes in the power of community and is ready to take the steps to build one that truly matters.

Enjoy the journey. You're in excellent hands.

ACKNOWLEDGEMENTS

There is no such thing as writing a book completely on your own. Writing my first ever book has probably been one of the hardest things I've done to this day, and it wouldn't have been possible without the help and support of all the wonderful people I'm lucky to surround myself with.

Firstly, thank you to my family, Amr and Amina. People usually wrap up with a 'last but not least', but I'm putting you right up top. Thank you for providing me with all the space I needed to write this book. I love you very much, and I am eternally grateful to have you both in my life.

My business partner and one of my very favourite people in the world, Erin Simmons. It took me a long time to find you. Building a community on my own felt extremely lonely until our paths crossed. Thank you for saying yes to being part of this journey with me. I learn so much from you every day.

Thank you to the Kogan Page team. Donna Goddard-Skinner, thank you for seeing something in me that I didn't see in myself and giving me the confidence that I can do this. Jeylan Ramis, thank you for your patience, feedback and encouragement.

Richard Millington, your knowledge of community marketing is second to none. Thank you for agreeing to write my book's Foreword, what an absolute honour.

Thank you to the brilliant people I interviewed and spoke with while writing this book: Alan Moir, Christina Garnett, Joel Gascoigne, Joelle Irvine, Knut Melvær, Laura Roth, and Pete Heslop. Without your valuable insights and your generosity in sharing your knowledge and experience, there would be no book. I appreciate each and every one of you very much.

Thank you to the wonderful community leaders who shared their learnings in this book: Amber Shand, Briony Cullin, Dan White, Emilia Gjorgjevska, Esme Verity, Fab Giovanetti, Jack Chambers-Ward, Jo Juliana Turnbull, Jo Walters, Julia Bocchese, Penni Pickering, Ruth Cheesley, Sarah Lewis and Yagmur Simsek.

Thank you to Arlo West, the best designer in the world, for saying yes to sketching the illustrations that can be found throughout this book.

My author support system, Allegra Chapman and Mo Kanjilal: fate had it that we were all writing our books at the same time. Being part of our WhatsApp group chat meant the world to me. I will forever be grateful for the support I received from you two. A massive shout out to your book, *The Inclusion Journey*, and all the brilliant work you do through Watch Th_s Space.

Hannah Smith, the mentorship you provided me with when I was struggling to put any words together will stay with me forever. Thank you for being a wonderful mentor and friend.

Alex Cassidy, you are one of the most talented writers I know, and lucky for me, you are also my very good friend. I appreciate all your encouragement and advice throughout this process. Flow State for the win!

I'm part of two communities that give me so much joy: Shine Crew and The Digital Marketing Union. Thank you to everyone in these groups for all their support.

I moved to the UK over a decade ago to find a new home, and thanks to the friendships that stayed with me, and the new ones I made, it truly did become my home. Thank you to every person I met along the way who made me feel like I belong.

Thank you to my own community: Women in Tech SEO. Thank you to every single community member, partner, sponsor and supporter. Thank you for being a kind, helpful, respectful and judgement-free space. Thank you for continuing to give and take, and for being the reason our community is the wonderful place it is.

Finally, thank YOU. Yes, you. For picking up my book, for supporting me and for trusting me with your time. I really hope that you find joy in reading this and that it gives you the inspiration you're seeking in your community journey.

Introduction

When I was eight, I created my very own magazine.

I called it 'Fun Magazine'.

It was a long, warm summer, and I was bored. I wanted to bring a magazine to life, where I would share entertaining news for my family to read. I thought it was a brilliant idea and that I would work on it forever.

With the help of Clippy on Microsoft Word, I used Word Art extensively and wrote several pages, ranging from the latest family news to quizzes, jokes and riddles.

My mum wasn't too pleased that I printed six magazine copies in colour. Looking back now, I can't say I blame her.

Still, I started working on the second issue right away, even though I hadn't received any requests for a need to work on another issue. I didn't print that one (having learned my lesson); instead, I asked everyone to crowd around the family computer to read it.

I dropped the magazine a week later because it felt like too much work. I informed my family that I was shutting down the publication and decided to spend the rest of my summer break playing computer games instead.

I now realize that was the first passion project I ever had.

Fast forward 10 years, I was juggling three passion projects alongside my university studies. The first was creating an academic programme, in my local library, for a cohort of 30 delegates, where I was one of five instructors. Our meetings took place once a week in person. We wanted to find a way to easily connect with our delegates during the week, to share resources and answer any questions they have. So, we created a private Facebook group to host us.

The second was working on our local Institute of Electrical and Electronics Engineers (IEEE) university chapter where we organized initiatives and events for our student members. We kept our members up to date with all our latest projects through an email newsletter and a private Google group.

The third was taking part in organizing the Egyptian Engineering Day (EED), an annual conference and expo for engineering graduation projects that welcomed thousands of attendees through the doors. I have the fondest memories of staying up till midnight with my team getting things set up for the morning registration rush.

Community is commonly defined as people who are considered as a social unit because of their shared interests.

I now realize that those were the first communities I took part in building.

I reflect on these memories and wonder: am I the right person to write this book?

I have not held any official 'community marketing' roles in companies. Yet, my unusual career path has led me into the role of a community founder, builder and leader purely off the back of a passion project of mine.

This project is my very own community, Women in Tech SEO (WTS), which I started in May 2019, at a point in my career where I no longer felt inspired or motivated. My specialism was Technical SEO, which stands for Search Engine Optimization, in the digital marketing industry. When people ask me why I started WTS, my answer is always honest, that it was purely selfish reasons. I was struggling to find a space where I felt like I belonged and one where I could ask questions without the fear of being judged. So, I decided to create that space myself.

As of 2024, WTS is a global community with over 10,000 members. Our mission is to provide a safe, and judgement-free space for people of marginalized genders in the marketing and tech space and help connect them with one another.

Our initiatives are free for our members and include our online community groups, workshops, newsletters and mentorship programmes. We host our international in-person conference, WTSFest, in London, Berlin, Philadelphia, Portland and Melbourne, with new locations being announced each year.

I regularly speak at conferences and panels on the importance of community marketing. One of the most common questions I get asked is how you can go about transforming an initial idea into a thriving community.

My hope is for this book to share exactly that, following a three-stage process that makes up our first three sections:

1 Launching your community

2 Growing your community

3 Scaling your community

I share with you all my learnings from the past few years; distilled into actionable and practical frameworks that you can apply to your communities. And you won't only be hearing from me. I spent hours interviewing CEOs, leaders and managers of companies who are running successful community-first companies, such as Buffer, Sanity, The TEFL Org and more. We will dive into their stories, as well as hear from community builders on their key learnings, to help put everything into practice. This book is packed with first-hand experience from leaders who have seen and done it all.

This is the book I wish I'd read when I first started my community.

Whether your community is still in its early days or has been around for a while and needs a boost, my goal is to help you capitalize on the opportunities that community marketing offers; transforming your customers from passive consumers to active, engaged brand advocates.

So, let's get started!

PART ONE
Launching your community

Finding your why

1

Let's start from the beginning.

You've heard about brands getting good results from building communities, and you're wondering if this approach would work for you. More than that, you want to know how to make it work for you. Well, before we dive into the details, we're going to take a step back and look at what we really mean when we talk about community.

In this chapter, we'll explore the nature of community, and what it means for marketers. We'll examine how your business might benefit from a community, how your organization might facilitate one and why you might create one.

What is community?

There are many different concepts of what a community is, and various definitions. Outside the context of marketing terminology, the word 'community' is primarily associated with local areas or neighbourhoods. The concept of community as a marketing or growth tool is one that only really began to gain traction in the 21st century.

When I first launched my own community, Women in Tech SEO, which I will refer to in this book as WTS, I didn't use the term 'community'. I used words like 'group' or 'network', but neither term felt quite right. As the language around community marketing became more common, I realized that this was, indeed, what I was creating – this word felt like a much more natural fit.

Definition of community

The general definition of community is twofold, firstly reflecting that older concept of location or identity as the unifying element:

> A group of people living in the same place or sharing a specific characteristic.

A second definition points to our newer interpretation of people coming together in a way that does not need to be physical, but where they are bonded more by ideas and passions:

> Possessing or sharing certain attitudes and interests in common.

Our society has gradually moved away from location-based communities. Many of us rarely work in companies based within walking distance of our homes. We commute, we relocate, we move away to study and we choose where to retire.

The Digital Community Leaders Survey Report[1] defines communities as 'social groups that unite people who share common interests, values, and goals and foster a sense of belonging. The interactions and collaborations among members allow them to exchange ideas, experiences, creative content and resources while nurturing a shared identity and purpose.'

We are now more able than ever before to build relationships globally. The internet, social media, hybrid working and remote study options enable us to connect with people anywhere in the world. The people we look to connect with are those who share our interests and our outlook.

Our communities now look more like what David M Chavis and Kien Lee describe as 'not a place, a building, or an organization… Community is both a feeling and a set of relationships among people.'[2]

At its heart, though, the nature of community hasn't changed. Fabian Pfortmüller, co-founder of the Together Institute, describes a community as 'a group of people that care about each other and feel they belong together'.[3] Whether these people are brought together by geography, by a sense of identity or by a passion for a particular interest, this essence of caring and belonging remains core to their view of themselves as a community.

What does a community look like?

Communities can take on many forms and formats.

They might come together in person or online, or in a combination of the two. They might be concentrated in a particular area, or spread around a country, continent or the whole world.

Communities are bonded together by something they have in common. This might be working in a certain profession or sector, or for a particular organization. It might be a shared interest or hobby. It could be that they all use a particular tool or product.

There are lots of different focal points around which a community can be built. The key is that enough people care enough about that thing to want to connect with other people that also care about it, and to talk to them about it.

As we've seen above, community is all about relationships. There needs to be a sense of connection, both to the topic and to the other members, in order for these individuals to become a community.

In 2022, Allie Volpe wrote an article in *Vox* on 'Why community matters so much',[4] and referenced the research on 'Sense of Community'[5] done by David W McMillan and David M Chavis, which suggests that a community is defined by four criteria:

- **Membership** – to feel a sense of belonging through shared identity, purpose or reason for being in the group
- **Influence** – to feel like you make a difference to the group and that the group makes a difference to you
- **Integration and fulfilment of needs** – to feel like your needs will be met by other group members
- **Shared emotional connection** – to feel that you share history or similar experiences

If your community members don't feel any of these things, then your community breaks down – essentially you don't have a community at all.

In this book, we'll touch on all the above, but the primary focus will be on the membership criteria; communities that are bonded by shared interests and activities that marketers can bring together in a way that is relevant to their business.

In community marketing, the brand exists largely in the background. Convening a community around a particular topic establishes you as an expert and leader in this area, and forms a close relationship with the community members, who are likely to be members of your target audience. But a relationship is not one-way – you should each get value from one another.

What is community marketing?

Community is not a synonym for customers. In building a community, you are not simply gathering together a group of people that you can sell to. Some of your community members may be customers, or may go on to become customers, but others will not. Some of your customers will never be interested in joining your community.

When you attract a customer, you are looking specifically for someone who wants to buy your product or service, and you then try to nurture a long-term relationship with them where they continue to buy from you.

When you attract a community member, you are inviting someone to become part of an ecosystem of which you are just one part. They will connect with you and the other members of the community. They may share attributes in common with your target customer, or they may be linked in other ways with your area of focus.

As counterintuitive as that may sound, the goal of a community is not to turn members into customers. The value of a member is not in whether they spend money with you. They may become advocates for you, recruit new community members and help new people get to know your brand. They may provide useful insights to you and your members, or they may become partners with whom you can collaborate.

You probably already have defined personas of your ideal customers. But, when it comes to community marketing, don't fall into the trap of thinking these are the personas you want to attract to your community. Consider the wider environment you want to create, and who would want to be part of that. Who could make a valuable contribution?

With marketing, we create blogs, videos, social media posts, FAQs, email newsletters, guides and resources that our target customers simply consume. With a community, on the other hand, we are building interactive relationships. This feels much more personable, and you connect with your members on a more human level. You get to know them as real people.

In my interview with Christina Garnett, fractional chief customer officer and advisor, whose expertise spans Fortune 500 companies to startups, she noted how many brands mistakenly try to use their communities as customer audiences. 'There's plenty of SaaS products that have "communities", but people are selfish and they're not giving, or they'll be like, "I can answer that question, but you need to set up time with me. You can't get to pick my brain". Whereas in the HubSpot community where I used to work, people will just tell you exactly how you do it. "Oh, this is the code I use for that" or "This is exactly the steps that I would take in order to create this if I were you". There's this inherent generosity. Yes, it's a part of the strategy, but so much of what makes the HubSpot community so unique and special is that the people in it are incredibly brilliant and generous.'

For HubSpot, the impact of nurturing these relationships is incredibly powerful. This goes beyond good customer service to drive brand advocates – community members are not only advocates for HubSpot, but they actively advise people on getting set up on the platform. Christina says, 'I get to be in a position where the fans that I work with, they don't just love us. They're deeply, deeply knowledgeable. They're power users. They're able to not just say, "Oh, you should pick HubSpot." They can intelligently expand on that: "Here's why you should and here's how you could, and here's how I would do that if I were you", which is incredibly helpful, instead of just rattling off a brand name.'

To get to that point, though, requires dedication. A community marketer needs to be continually serving their community, and constantly thinking about how to improve it. You need to understand what your members want from the space and from you. What are their needs, their concerns and their frustrations, in the context of your community topic? Where can you help them, and where are they currently struggling to get help from you? When you show your members that you care about them, you demonstrate that this is a real community, not a sales platform, and a space where they can belong.

As Christina says, 'There are very few things in marketing you can set and leave, and community is something you can't. You can build it, and they will come, but if you don't keep working on it, it will feel like you've led them all into a room and left them there, which is not a good experience.'

Benefits of community for brands

So, with all this effort involved, why is it worth investing in community building? At a time when we're all working hard to build social media followings and email lists, is this just another platform to have to try to grow?

Unlike your social media followers and email subscribers, your community members are in a close relationship with you. They are rooting for you, brainstorming with you, helping you to uncover ideas and opportunities, and willing you to succeed.

Community members will often be the first to share new products and services that you release – they actively amplify and promote your brand for you because they feel as though they're part of something. They can also be actively on the lookout for potential customers whom they will knowledgeably persuade to join you, even helping to onboard these people for you.

They provide valuable insights into what new features, products or services you need to create and where certain elements might need refining or adjusting. They will be your beta testers and troubleshooters. They help you understand how to craft your messaging because regular conversations with your community will let you see how your potential customers talk about your product or your industry and what they are looking for.

When you have direct access to a community, it can take minutes to get insights, as opposed to requiring large-scale research projects that may take months to extract valuable information from your target customers.

'For too long we've seen consumerism push brands into unsustainable growth models,' says Pete Heslop, Managing Director of Steadfast Collective. For the past decade, Pete and his team have built bespoke platforms that enable community-led brands to thrive. Pete believes that community is foundational for regenerative business growth.

'We've taken responsibility to provide an alternative,' Pete says, 'Steadfast Collective believes that people thrive when gathered in community; that generative places, spaces and platforms are where communities grow.'

The Digital Community Leaders Survey Report[6] states that communities help individuals, organizations and society thrive by enabling knowledge sharing, collaboration and the cocreation of value.

The report goes on to highlight that digital communities play an increasingly essential role in 21st-century lives, organizations and societies. They affect business outcomes. Today, brands 'earn loyalty and growth' by participating in them. The report also highlights that communities 'lessen reliance on costly marketing campaigns and traditional customer support methods'. And that 'empowering customers within online communities cultivates a feeling of ownership, leading to user-generated content, valuable insights, and peer support'.

The report also states that a majority of 70 per cent online communities have grown over the last 12 months, and some of the factors driving this growth include:

- The shift to life online
- The normalization of content creation and sharing
- The desire for brands to access customer feedback directly

Community goes far beyond brand awareness or engagement – it's the next level of retention and loyalty.

'Community gives you a competitive edge. It really can't be replicated,' says Laura Roth, B2B SaaS community and marketing leader. With experience managing communities at Amazon, WeWork and Vodafone, Laura knows just how impactful the benefits are. But she also knows that, to achieve those benefits, you need to put in the work. You need to create something unique, that comes from your specific mission and values as an organization, and that speaks to the particular needs of your community. 'Community is a long-term game,' Laura says, 'it doesn't happen overnight, and you can't copy it.'

If you're not prepared to invest the time, then you won't see the outcome.

Internal communities

We often think about community as something you build externally, but your organization's sense of community starts internally.

As we will see later in this chapter, your team will be leading and facilitating your community, so they need to be rooted in the vision and values that you are looking to instil. But they are also the first wave of advocates for your brand, and the people with the most in-depth knowledge about your company. You want to harness them, not only to build your external community, but to become a community in themselves.

When your internal team has a sense of belonging, that they care about one another and about the business, then they are more likely to stay in their jobs for longer and to give more of their best work to that job.

As Christina Garnett says, many companies have made a lot of loud noise about community, only to lay off substantial numbers of their team a year later. Not only does this damage trust among your internal staff, it doesn't do much to convince your external audience that you mean what you say about your commitment to community.

Long-term commitment

As both Christina and Laura have noted, community does not yield overnight results. Relationships take time – you don't become best friends over a 30-minute phone call.

If you're considering setting up a community because you think this is a buzzword to be checked off or a trend to follow, then your community will not flourish and will not deliver value.

The good news is that that commitment goes both ways. When you commit to the relationship, your members do too. Community makes customers sticky. Leaving your brand no longer simply means leaving your tool or service; it means leaving all the people, resources, events and experiences within that community. It's much harder to say goodbye.

Relationships are powerful sales tools, too. People buy from people. We all prefer to do business with people we like, and if we become part of a community where we feel welcomed and supported, then we are more inclined to do business with the brand behind it.

'Every community is about how you can make somebody feel a different way,' Christina says. It's about building relationships where everyone cares about each other.

Impact of the pandemic

In recent years, the number of companies talking about community and investing in community marketing has substantially risen. While this has certainly evolved from the growth of social media and online community spaces, most of the community marketers I spoke to in the research for this book talked about the impact of the pandemic.

When Covid-19 forced us into lockdowns and social distancing, people craved connection. As they searched for spaces to come together, new tools emerged to meet this need.

Webinar, video-conferencing and online collaboration tools improved dramatically during this period, as demand and usage increased. It became more accessible and easier to bring people together in online spaces.

The pandemic also made businesses realize that they couldn't rely purely on in-person connections, and that they didn't have to be restricted to their local areas. They set about considering how to reach a global audience more easily and effectively.

In a time where many companies were facing desperate circumstances, they were more willing to experiment, try different things and be more open with their audiences. This yielded valuable results, and the power of community building was revealed.

Now online collaboration and virtual meetings are second nature. Even now that lockdowns are (hopefully) behind us, most events and conferences ensure they have a form of online presence, such as recording or live streaming their sessions. Not only does this allow them to capture a larger audience, but it also makes events far more accessible for those who can't attend in person, are based in a different location, or have access needs.

The pandemic brought community front of mind for many organizations and individuals, forcing it to become a greater focus.

As Christina says, 'Covid was definitely an inflection point. It changed user behaviours on a core level that we've never seen.' Not only that, but, as Christina notes, a lot of companies are now very aware of the impact of loneliness, which was thrown into sharp contrast by the pandemic, and are now looking to address that. Of course, for some businesses that's about simply cashing in on a trend, but Christina says the way to spot those is to see how long they stick with it. 'The real people who care will beat the drum after the hype cycle's over. The people who are left standing are the ones who actually care and are continuing to beat that drum. I think the hype cycle for community, it's not completely over, but it's definitely cresting. When AI took over, community was like, okay, well, you all can have it. We're fine.'

Where community fits in an organization

A good community can touch every part of a business.

You may initially create your community with a specific purpose in mind, but you will likely find that its impact will spread far beyond the function of the organization you had in mind. It's, therefore, worth taking a holistic view of the different elements of your business and how the community might relate to each one.

Who takes the lead?

It's very common for responsibility for the community to be given to the marketing department, but that might not always necessarily be the best approach. In a tech company, for example, the community might most effectively be led by teams with the most in-depth understanding of the product or service so that they can provide the best possible support and guidance, and so that they speak the language of your members. Sanity, a company we will meet in Chapter 13, has built a community that aims to connect developers with one another, so it was evident to them that their community should be led by developers.

For The TEFL Org, however, community falls very much within the marketing function, because this is the team that creates the content and resources that answer the community's questions and serves their needs. We will learn more about their community in Chapter 12.

Buffer, on the other hand (we'll dive into their story in Chapter 14), has a community steering group comprised of representatives of every department. This means that there is input from every area of the business, and a relationship with the community that spans the entire company. Whatever questions come from the community, it also means that there is an expert available on that particular area who can supply an answer.

There is no one-size-fits-all approach to community, and the way that your community relates to your organization and the different roles that people in your business take in facilitating your community will depend on your specific needs and goals.

What different roles might you need?

There are a range of different roles that people within your organization might take in relation to your community. Here are a few of them, and what their responsibilities might entail.

- **Community Lead:** Oversees the community as a whole and decides on its strategic direction
- **Community Manager:** Manages the day-to-day running of the community and develops its guidelines
- **Community Moderator:** Monitors discussions and enforces community rules
- **Community Ambassador:** Represents the community externally and helps bring in new members

Who takes on these roles?

Most of the community experts that I interviewed for this book didn't initially look for a community role. Very few people spend their entire careers in community – most find themselves moving into this work almost without realizing it. They might come from marketing backgrounds, or from specialist roles, and find that community offers them a powerful opportunity to achieve their objectives.

Laura Roth talked to me about a search conference she was involved in organizing, where they wanted to set up networking opportunities during the breaks, and Laura was determined to do something different.

'The idea was that there would be topic-led tables, and each one would be led by a sponsor and a speaker. People could just walk around during the session and sit down at any table, and they were supposed to direct the conversation. We would put a few prompts in there, but it was just this idea of being able to actually talk about a topic. We asked ourselves, how do we actually create this space for people to connect with each other more? Because when you're watching a conference, you're not really connecting with people.

'We created a space where people would meet people, one-on-one, that were interested in the same topics, and that had a huge impact on how that whole thing went. I don't think I realized at the time that this was community building, but it was, and it's the greatest way, really. It was a natural community-building space.'

While many of the people I spoke to hadn't sought out a community role, they were naturally drawn to this work because they wanted to bring people together and foster connection between them.

Christina says that a lot of her career has involved non-traditional functions, but, looking back, her roles always in some way involved connecting people. Her work often involved acting as a bridge, whether that be brand to people or people to people.

Christina's first introduction to community was working as a career services advisor for a technical school. There weren't many opportunities for alumni to connect or maintain a relationship with the organization, and, because the school had been through a rebrand, former students were identified as being part of two completely separate groups depending on when they graduated. The first thing that Christina did was to create an alumni page on LinkedIn and begin to bring those separate groups together.

'This created an alumni network for them, so they would be able to connect with each other and have opportunities to really chat instead of only connecting when they needed something,' Christina explains. 'Because traditionally, in my role, they would only reach out to me when they needed a job. There are other ways that we could take care of them beyond just getting them hired somewhere else. That'd probably be my first official "got paid to do community" thing. Then I've done a lot with social. I tend to be a bit protective on social. I don't like it when it's used for bad. I like it when it's used to connect people.'

Social media is a big passion for Christina, and this natural passion has led to it becoming a major component of her work, building networks with people online who she can connect with in an authentic way. 'I've learned in my life that throwing rocks at giants doesn't work,' she tells me. 'The people who think they're great, there's nothing you could do or say, there's no tweet that you could find and show them. They're all in regardless. I've learned that it's just better to amplify the good. I hope I'm a bit of a champion for the smaller creators, the people who are doing really great work and maybe don't have a ton of followers, but they're saying really great things and they're doing really good work, and they need to be seen. I find that instead of throwing rocks at giants, I just tend to amplify the smaller creators until they're not small anymore.'

One of Christina's first community moves on social came off the back of a December 2020 post on X, formerly known as Twitter,[7] that went viral. It stated that if you have less than 1,000 followers and work in marketing in some capacity, introduce yourself and she'll help amplify that to her followers.

She was inspired to write the tweet because of the number of people she saw devaluing themselves: 'I find a lot of people, especially in the marketing community space, we self-reject a lot,' she says. 'We look for ways to make sure that we don't qualify. Most people, especially on social, they want to connect with others, but they don't want to be dragged, they don't want to be ridiculed, they don't want to be, basically, dismissed and rejected. A lot of people in social, they want a door. That's why social media chats were a really great thing because it encourages people, regardless of their following, to be a part of the conversation.'

It's important to remember that everyone starts somewhere, and it's thanks to people like Christina, who amplify people early on in their journeys, that individuals can grow communities. When we reach a place where we have substantial followings and networks, we should remember to give back.

Christina says that to this day, she still receives replies to that original tweet, and she's still connected to a lot of people that responded originally. 'I know people who've gotten jobs because of people they connected to. I know people who have best friends that they found in that chat, people who've dated because it's deeply connected, which is really lovely.

'Then before that tweet went viral, I was already talking to HubSpot about joining their team because I'd been a HubSpot fan for ages. I'd owned my own consulting firm where I'd worked with HubSpot agencies on social strategy, and I'd been attending INBOUND [HubSpot's annual conference] since 2016. I was in the ecosystem already. I was brought in to revive an advocacy programme called HubStars that never really hit as hard as it could have. There were some core people who loved it, but it never flourished. I worked with the community team to make sure that it was intersectioned, and so they're not competing with each other. If anything, we feed off each other and we're able to be mutually beneficial. That launched in 2021 and is still going strong.'

Communication across the business

Although you might have a dedicated team responsible for managing your community, it's important that an understanding of and relationship with the community doesn't end with this team.

You want to create lines of communication across the organization, so that different teams are aware of what's happening in the community and can provide their own input. This means every team can add value to the community, and they can all take learnings from it.

This will take careful crafting of processes and mechanisms to enable that communication. You will need to help each department to understand the way that your community works and how they might be able to both utilize and contribute to it. Regular check-ins with each team will allow you to share insights that might be useful and find out what each team is working on that might be relevant to the community.

We talk more about how to measure the success of your community and communicate it to relevant stakeholders in Chapter 11.

Why do you need a community?

Every community has a 'why' behind it.

In the next chapter, we'll look at how you define the vision and mission for your community, but first, let's start with why you're looking at creating one in the first place.

From a brand perspective, your 'why' might be solving a problem for your audience or offering support and connection within your industry. It comes from understanding where people within your space are encountering pain points, and recognizing where you are able to help.

Your 'why' needs to be your guiding light that directs the actions and approach you take. As Laura Roth says, 'It's easy to forget your why along the way, and it's something that's worth revisiting, to make sure that it doesn't get lost. It's something that people have to keep going back to. You might start off with a "why", but that changes a few months down the line. People don't realize when they've gone away from their why, they forget why they're building what they're building. It's important to remember what you were trying to do. What's the point of building your community in the first place? If you don't have an answer to that question, you may end up doing things for the sake of doing things, but not actually adding any value to anyone.'

Personally, my motivation to start my community, WTS, came from feeling discouraged and demotivated in an industry to which I had dedicated many years. I didn't feel represented. I didn't feel like I was part of something, I didn't feel that I fitted in. So, I made the conscious choice to create my own group where I could belong, and where others who were feeling a similar way could also find that place of connection.

In a way, my 'why' was quite a selfish one! I built something that I, personally, needed. But it's inevitable that, if one person needs something, others will too. So once WTS began, it became clear that others were having experiences like my own.

What's your 'why'?

It may feel daunting to write out your own 'why', but here is a three-step process to follow that can help you.

Step one: Answer the following three questions

1 Who is this community for?

2 What's the single, most compelling reason for people to join this community, focusing on what's in it for them?

3 What makes this community different?

Step two: Use your answers to the above questions to draft your 'why' statement

Step three: Check/review/validate

- Does your why statement clearly communicate **who** this community is for?
- Does your why statement clearly state the **reason** people should join, and what's in it for them?
- Does your why statement clearly articulate what **differentiates** your community from others?

It may take several iterations until you come up with a why statement that feels right for you. But this will be a statement that you continue to revisit throughout your time growing and scaling your community, and you'll find yourself leaning on it when making big decisions.

In the next chapter, we'll look at how you can take this 'why' and shape it into a vision and mission, as well as a set of values that will bring those to life.

Key takeaways

- Community is about building relationships and a sense of connection.
- Communities can take on many forms and can be built around many different types of focal point – in this book, we are focusing on communities built around shared interests, activities or professions that marketers can bring together to align with brand objectives.

- Your community are not your customers – don't make the mistake of trying to sell to your members or thinking they only have value if they are buying from you.
- There are many different benefits of communities for brands, including providing you with valuable insights and vocal, and persuasive, advocates.
- These benefits take long-term commitment and investment in the relationship.
- When customers do become part of your community, this makes them 'sticky' and more likely to stay with you long term.
- There are different ways that your community can be facilitated, which will depend on the needs of your business and your audience, and on what you are trying to achieve.
- You need to be clear on why you are building a community, and keep revisiting your 'why' over time.

Reflection questions

In thinking about the 'why' behind your community, spend some time reflecting on the following questions.

1 What does community mean to you?
2 Why would your organization benefit from building a community?
3 What value would your community offer to its members?

Notes

1 Digital Community Leaders. 2023 Digital Community Leaders Survey Report, 2023, https://digitalcommunityleaders.com/ (archived at https://perma.cc/BU3S-H336)
2 D M Chavis and K Lee. What is community anyway? 12 May 2015, Stanford Social Innovation Review, https://ssir.org/articles/entry/what_is_community_anyway (archived at https://perma.cc/FRM8-PQQY)

3 F Pfortmüller. What does 'community' even mean? A definition attempt and conversation starter, Medium, 20 September 2017, https://medium.com/together-institute/what-does-community-even-mean-a-definition-attempt-conversation-starter-9b443fc523d0 (archived at https://perma.cc/KX3E-ZYWC)

4 A Volpe. Why community matters so much – and how to find yours, *Vox*, 24 March 2022, www.vox.com/22992901/how-to-find-your-community-as-an-adult (archived at https://perma.cc/6F9H-GT4T)

5 D V McMillan and D M Chavis. An Introduction to Sense of the Community, nd, www.drdavidmcmillan.com/sense-of-community/article-1 (archived at https://perma.cc/H56M-ZWWS)

6 Digital Community Leaders. 2023 Digital Community Leaders Survey Report, 2023, https://digitalcommunityleaders.com/ (archived at https://perma.cc/275F-E4C5)

7 C Garnett @ThatChristinaG. X, 3 December 2020, https://x.com/ThatChristinaG/status/1334486296018948102 (archived at https://perma.cc/8SYZ-5KFB)

Defining your culture

2

One of the most common ways that new communities go wrong is by rushing into building the platform without first thinking about why this community is being created in the first place. Any organization needs a clear vision and mission, along with defined values and a plan of action – a community is no different. So, in this chapter, we'll look at how you can put these fundamental elements in place from the start so that your community will be built on solid foundations.

If you start creating a community without clarity on these key factors, you risk creating something that neither your business nor your audience needs, and that isn't serving you or them. You may also end up with a platform that isn't aligned with your business objectives, or what you stand for as an organization. When you take the time to get this step right, you can build a community that supports your wider goals, offers real value to your audience, and works in harmony with your day-to-day objectives.

Laying the foundations

Your organization was set up with a vision (the long-term impact it aims to have, or contribute to, on the world) and a mission (the shorter-term goals it sets out to achieve). It will also likely have a list of core values that determine how it goes about pursuing those goals, and helps potential employees and customers/clients understand whether this is an organization they want to connect with. These may evolve over time, likely with input from your internal and external audience, as the landscape that you operate within shifts, but these elements remain the foundations on which your company is built.

Your community needs these elements, too. As with any project, you need to know why you're doing it and what you want to achieve before you start. A clear vision and mission not only helps you understand what you need to build in order to address your objectives, but they also help to attract members to your community by showing them what they would be part of, and giving them a compelling reason to join. If you are going to invite a wide variety of external people to come together and connect with one another, they're going to need to understand why they should and what they will get out of it.

Just as your organization's values attract employees and customers by helping them understand whether they are aligned with you, your community's values tell the right target audience that this is a place where they can belong. They set the parameters for the culture that should exist within your community. Alongside these values, you'll need a set of rules that prevent conflict and enable you to take action when issues arise.

These elements aren't just about deciding what you want – they're also about what you don't want. By being clear on your vision, mission and values, and having clear rules that everyone understands, you know where your focus should be, and what you should avoid being sidetracked by; you know who you want to attract into your community, and whose presence wouldn't benefit you or them; and you know what behaviour you want to encourage, and what behaviour won't be tolerated.

Knowing what you want and don't want might help you make a decision on the final key foundational element – monetization. Whether you offer a free, freemium or paid community is a big decision, and can often be a confusing one. So in this chapter, we'll look in detail at the different options and which might be suitable for your needs.

It can be tempting to skip this stage and get stuck straight into building the community, but I urge you to invest the time and energy now. It will be much harder to go back and try to reverse engineer these important elements later. These are your anchors, clarifying your path forward on this journey. They bring your community to life, attracting, energizing and engaging your audience. They also hold both you and your members accountable. It's worth getting them right from the beginning.

Let's look at each of our foundational blocks in detail.

Vision and mission

The words 'vision' and 'mission' are often used interchangeably in business, but they mean different things.

Vision – what you would like to see happen in the long term

Mission – what you are working towards right now to contribute towards this vision

To give you a sense of the difference, here are a few examples.

IKEA

Vision – To create a better everyday life for the many people.

Mission – To offer a wide range of well-designed, functional home furnishing products at prices so low that as many people as possible will be able to afford them.[1]

IKEA's big vision is to be part of a positive change in society, influencing both individual happiness and sustainable behaviours that will help the planet.

To work towards this vision, their mission is to create affordable home furnishing products, making stylish and sustainable items accessible to a wide range of people.

Southwest Airlines

Vision – To become the world's most loved, most flown, and most profitable airline.

Mission – The mission of Southwest Airlines is dedication to the highest quality of customer service delivered with a sense of warmth, friendliness, individual pride, and company spirit.[2]

American airline Southwest has an ambitious vision to be the most popular airline in the world, and they are pursuing that goal by focusing their mission on providing the best possible customer service.

Amazon

Vision – To be Earth's most customer-centric company.

Mission – To continually raise the bar of the customer experience by using the internet and technology to help consumers find, discover and buy anything, and empower businesses and content creators to maximize their success.[3]

Amazon's long-term vision is to be more customer-focused than any other company on the planet, and so it makes sense that their mission should be to keep looking for ways to improve customer experience and selection.

Defining your vision and mission

The vision for your community may well be linked to the vision for your organization. It is helpful here to think about why both exist. What long-term impact would you like to see in the world? What change would you like to contribute towards in your world/local community/industry?

Before you begin to create your community, consider what end goal you believe that its existence can help work towards. This really brings your community to life when you see it as part of a much bigger goal, and a possible future.

Then, once you know what larger change you are seeking, you can consider what your community can do right now to help make that happen. What actions would lead to the kind of impact you want to see? What needs to be done differently to fulfil this need?

The vision and mission need to unite your team and the external people who will become members of this community, so bringing multiple people together to define these key elements is important. You might find it useful to bring your team together, possibly with some representatives of your target audience, for a brainstorming session to explore the following questions:

Vision

- What is the problem or challenge we are trying to solve?
- What impact would we like to see 10 years from now?
- What does our audience most care about?
- What would happen if this community was never built?
- Why does this matter?

Mission

- What is happening in our area/industry that is leading to this problem/challenge?
- What needs to be done differently?
- What can we do to influence the situation?
- What can we do that no one else can do/is doing?
- What is the first step towards the long-term impact we're looking for?

The reality of vision and mission

My personal story of learning how to put all this together is quite different.

The vision doesn't always come first. In a brand-new community, particularly one that isn't led by a business with an existing vision, it's normal to initially identify the mission, before getting an understanding of your long-term vision. With Women in Tech SEO (WTS), I began with the mission 'to connect and amplify women through a safe community where we can support one another'. This was something that I recognized a real need for, as a woman in a highly male-dominated industry, where women often felt silenced and sidelined. So, my initial approach centred on what I could do to address that issue.

Over time, the vision was formed from people asking me, 'Where do you see WTS five years down the line?' When I reflected on this question, the answer helped me come up with our vision: I see a world where the community is no longer needed, because, if we've done all the work that needs to be done, and the industry is finally in a good place, then this work should be deemed redundant.

The vision for our community, then, is to contribute to a position where our industry is inclusive, welcoming, fair, kind and non-judgemental; where safe spaces for underrepresented groups are no longer needed, because everywhere feels like a safe space.

Five years down the line of WTS, when we sat down to officially write out our vision and mission on paper, we found it extremely difficult. I think there's a pressure that may come with such strict terminology. So, my brilliant managing director, Erin Simmons, suggested we answer the following instead:

- Who we are
- Why we are
- What we want
- How we get there

We found those much easier to answer, and it felt like a much more natural way to describe WTS.

In 2024, this is what we wrote down.

Who we are

A community for people of marginalized genders in marketing and tech

Why we are

People of marginalized genders have historically experienced a lack of belonging in SEO, marketing and tech

What we want

A future where all people feel a true sense of belonging through community

How we get there

By creating a recipe of belonging built on centring diverse voices and providing them with opportunities, connection, amplification and education.

If we wanted to translate that into a typical Vision and Mission statement, it would likely look something like this:

Vision – A world where people feel a true sense of belonging through community.

Mission – To create a recipe of belonging built on centring diverse voices and providing them with opportunities, connection, amplification and education.

In essence, it says the same thing, but using a Who/Why/What/How framework felt a lot more like us, and that's what matters most, for your community to feel authentic.

Values

While your vision is the long-term impact you want to see, and your mission is what you are going to do now to work towards that, your organizational values govern how you will go about doing that work. Your values define the way that you act and how you expect everyone (staff and customers) to treat one another.

Similarly, your community values are the standards that guide the way you run the community. The values of your community should be aligned with those of your business, because these are going to tell people whether you are a good fit for them. Your customers want to know what you stand for before they choose to do business with you, and your community members will want to know the same before they make a connection. Since you want these people to be from the same groups, you want to make sure you're attracting the right tribe.

In the same way that your company values build your organizational culture, by showing your staff how they should behave and take action, your community values build the culture that will shape the offline and/or online spaces you create. Everyone in your community needs to be aware of these so that they know what is expected of them, and what they can expect from you and each other. You want your values to be front of mind in conversations and discussion points, and in events and meetups.

You also need to ensure that your team is modelling those values, both to show community members how they are lived in practice and to ensure that this approach becomes embedded within the community. This isn't always easy at first. In my interview with Laura Roth, B2B SaaS community and marketing leader, we talked about how it takes time and training for staff to get used to being less corporate and more natural in the way they embody the values of the community. The last thing you want is for your staff to approach your community as a sales channel – this is a trap that a lot of communities fall into, and it instantly turns off members. So how can you encourage staff to show up in a way that is aligned with your values and doesn't make people feel they're constantly being sold to?

'You don't put words in their mouth,' Laura says. 'I sometimes say to my team members, "if you want to post something in our community and you're not sure, just message me and I'll tell you what I think", but you don't want to tell them [what to post] because it needs to sound authentic. I think that's sometimes when you need to make them realize, just be yourself, because that is the best way to do it: be yourself and be chatty. Chat on there how you would chat to a friend in a social setting, because otherwise, it's really obvious when someone isn't authentic and they're trying to be someone else.'

This is where the values of your organization become so important because, if you have clearly defined the culture of your company and attracted employees who are aligned with those values, it will come more easily to them to live those values in interactions with community members. This, in turn, makes community members feel more included and that they belong.

As Laura explains, the values you model internally also influence the way your team shows up in the community space. 'I've had it where I've responded to someone internally, and they didn't respond back to me, and I was like, "Listen, we have to model the behaviour that we want to see. If you don't do that, other people are going to follow the same thing. You might think, that's just me, it's not really important, because it's not someone external, but somebody else is looking at that and thinking, *if she posted and didn't get a response, maybe I'm a bit scared, I won't bother*, and then that starts to show that habit." You do need to spend some time with internal teams so that they realize that you can model that behaviour.'

It's vital that your community feels that they will be respected and heard when they contribute to conversations, and ensuring that your staff feel the same is a good way to start that ripple effect.

Code of conduct

Your vision, mission and values are critical – but your code of conduct is truly what can make or break your community. Your code of conduct governs the everyday running of your community, and a clearly defined conduct ensures that your members can uphold it in every interaction they have inside your community space.

Setting the rules

The rules are the practical guide to how your values are lived in different circumstances. These tell everyone exactly what is expected of them and what is and is not acceptable within the community.

Most communities have rules, especially in online spaces. When you create a Facebook group, you are even given a set of template rules by default, which you can amend or add to, to suit your needs; in a way these are your set of governing guidelines. Online spaces are particularly susceptible to negative behaviour, as you can have a very wide-ranging group of people brought together, who may not know each other in an offline capacity, and some may not be using a real identity. People behave very differently in online spaces, which feel

Figure 2.1   Vision, mission, values, code of conduct

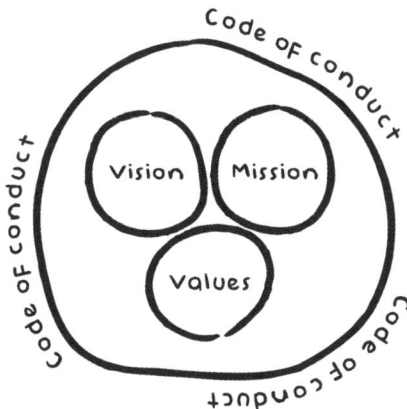

less real and more distant than an offline space where a real person is standing right in front of you, so they can require quite careful moderation. You may wish to have different rules for online and offline spaces that specifically address the needs of each.

When you have clear rules in place, you can ensure you moderate fairly. If someone has behaved in a way that contravenes the rules, then it is a straightforward matter for you to take action. You can point out the rule breach and remove any offending posts or content. You can either speak to the member to ask that they don't behave in this way again or, if you believe it is necessary or the action is serious enough, remove them from the community. Whatever course of action you take, you can point to the rule that has been broken in explaining your decision. Members also understand when they can come to you for help if someone is behaving in a way that clearly violates the rules.

Without clearly stated rules, it becomes very difficult for you to explain the rationale behind different actions, and it can be difficult for your team to know how to respond in complex situations.

Creating a code of conduct

You can use your rules, along with your values, to create a code of conduct. This is where you set out the behaviour you expect and set the tone for the culture you wish to build.

This should form part of your sign-up process – before a new member can join the community, they should agree to abide by the code of conduct.

This document needs to be shared with every member of your community, and attention should be drawn to it every time you hold an event or a meetup so that everyone knows what is expected of them, and what they can expect from being in your space.

Your code of conduct may include:

- Values
- Rules
- Guidelines on inclusive language

- Examples of behaviour that will not be tolerated (e.g. bullying, harassment, hate speech)
- What action will be taken if rules are broken
- How members can report actions that violate the rules

As with the elements above, your rules and code of conduct may evolve over time. It may become apparent that there is a need for a rule that you hadn't previously thought of, or new rules are necessary as the way your community runs develops. If you make any additions or changes to your rules or code of conduct, make sure that you communicate that loud and clear to your members.

Sanity's community code of conduct

Sanity's code of conduct[4] is an excellent one to reference as an example. It starts by explaining who this code of conduct applies to.

> All participants in the Sanity.io community must comply with the Sanity.io code of conduct. This includes discussions and contributions to GitHub repositories, our Slack workspace, meetups, events, and other venues hosted by Sanity.io. We're all on the same team and responsible for maintaining a welcoming community.

It then highlights a short version of the code of conduct at the top, for accessibility and ease, highlighting the parts that matter most, to ensure that most people read it.

The code of conduct is very readable, and includes the following headings:

- Expected behaviour
- Unacceptable behaviour
- Consequences of unacceptable behaviour
- Reporting

Now, most of the time, a community code of conduct seems to only highlight what's unacceptable, but Sanity took the time to also outline what's expected from their community members, which can be very powerful, as it also focuses on how members can abide by these rules and be helpful to one another.

The WTS Way

For WTS, our code of conduct is called The WTS Way,[5] and we reference it everywhere. When a member signs up, at the member onboarding stage, in our event speaker guide, we even include it in our freelancer contracts. We start by listing our community values.

✓ To be kind

✓ To be helpful

✓ To be respectful

✓ To be a safe and judgement-free community

These values are not just words, they're ones we abide by, and as a team, we ensure that we model those in every conversation and interaction we have, inside and outside the community.

Following that, in the code of conduct, we then highlight the focus of our community, to ensure everyone is aligned.

A FOCUS ON US AND OUR COLLECTIVE GOALS

Our community is a space for conversations and discussions that centre on our collective career goals of providing and receiving:

✓ Connections

✓ Education

✓ Amplification

✓ Opportunities

What you share in our community spaces should contribute to driving each other forward in our careers within these areas of focus.

The reason we specifically added this section to our code of conduct is because, at times, we felt some of the conversations in the community strayed away from the above, and we wanted to have a way to ensure that discussions that took place in the community focused on our collective career goals.

We then go on to highlight and break down the following sections:

- Community rules
- Anti-harassment
- Inclusive language
- Consent
- Enforcement
- Reporting

Our code of conduct has evolved over time, as we have seen a need for greater clarity or guidance. For example, after hosting our first few events, we realized that we needed to add points around inclusive language and consent, which we had not previously considered. We made sure these points were in place for future events and updated our community members every time we made changes to our code.

We're always learning, and it's important to remember that a code of conduct is not set in stone. It's difficult to predict and cater for all scenarios upfront, and new situations may arise where you realize the need to update your code.

Monetization model

Once you have those important building blocks in place, the final setup decision you have to make is on monetization. There are three main monetization models to choose from.

1 Free community
   As the name suggests, a free community is open for anyone to join, with no fees of any kind to pay.

2 Freemium
   The name 'freemium' is a portmanteau of the words 'free' and 'premium'. This model usually allows a basic level of access for

free and offers more advanced features or tools for a fee. It could also be that the community itself is free, but fees are required to access specific elements, such as workshops or events.

3 Paid community
Alternatively, you could choose to make the entire community accessible only to those who pay a fee. Fees are usually on a monthly or annual basis.

Access to your community could also be linked to your existing fee structure. If, for example, you offer a platform with different subscription models, a higher subscription tier might include access to your community.

There might be other requirements for joining, besides subscription fees. As Laura Roth says, 'They might have a barrier to entry; you have to be a customer, or they're open for people who aren't customers but maybe there's some elements within the community that are closed off or locked off for customers.'

As with all the other elements in this chapter, your approach to monetization may evolve. It is very common to start out with a free model, and then introduce a paid tier option later. This allows communities to grow a loyal and engaged membership more quickly, as people are enticed by the free access; then, once they have seen the value, they may be more willing to upgrade to a paid option.

On the other hand, sometimes a paid model can be attractive in its exclusivity. Then, once the community has gained a reputation, offering certain elements for free can drive demand from people who have become intrigued.

Any changes you make need to be well thought out, though, and you need to have a clear rationale behind your decision. There will likely be questions, and some of your members may not be too happy about the changes, so you'll need to be able to explain why you're making them.

Considerations for going paid

Laura notes that paying a fee can increase a member's engagement: 'I think there's an argument that if you pay for something, you are more actually inclined to go into it. You are a bit more invested in it. There's something about making something more exclusive that gets people a bit more interested, because we're finding that, with free events, sometimes people are less likely to come.'

Avoiding no-shows is a popular reason for asking people to pay, as free events are plagued by people who say they're coming and don't turn up. This can be very costly for event organizers. Users may also sign up for an app or platform, but then not bother to engage; whereas if they've paid money, they're more likely to get involved in your space.

You will have costs associated with your community, from software to event spaces, and charging fees can be a way to cover these costs.

Although Laura also warns that this might not be the most inclusive approach: 'I think there's another argument that maybe you are sidelining a few people and that people have to be in a certain position to be able to then come. Then are you really hitting the diversity aims? Because potentially you're just going after the privileged people who are able to pay. I think that's difficult. That's really difficult.' You want to avoid ending up with a community composed exclusively of one type of person, as diversity is key to driving engagement and productive discussions.

Choosing a paid model requires careful consideration. You will want to make space for a certain number of funded places for people who cannot afford the fees. You could also look at geographical-based pricing, which adjusts costs for different locations. This can mean adapting to local currencies, but also keeping costs lower for less socio-economically privileged areas.

If you are taking a freemium approach, you still need to ensure that you are providing something of value to your free members, not just focusing all your attention on your paid members.

How does a free community make money?

I get this question a lot, as someone who runs a free community. As a community, WTS has been free since day one, and I plan to keep it this way for our members. These are the two ways we currently make money.

- **Partnership programme**
  We have an official partnership programme, WTSPartner,[6] where brands and companies can enrol to get monthly shout-outs through our community groups and social media channels. We talk more about different forms of partnership in Chapter 9.
- **Conferences**
  We run our full-day conferences, WTSFest,[7] in London, Berlin, Philadelphia, Portland and Melbourne, with more locations being added every year, and we charge for ticket prices and sponsor slots. We talk more about events in Chapter 6.

It's also worth noting that we're set up as a social enterprise, which means that we have a legal commitment to reinvest at least half of our profits back into our organization to further our mission.

Every community is different. As a brand, running a free community can easily be a marketing expense that you absorb, because of how valuable its impact is.

Can these things change?

It may feel intimidating to work on your vision, mission and values, especially if you plan to put them out in the world and share them with your community members. Something about it feels very final. But change is normal, and you may decide down the line to make some changes to these elements, especially once your community scales and its trajectory goes in a different direction than what you initially planned for. What matters most is how you communicate these changes with your members. We talk about navigating change in detail in Chapter 10.

In the next chapter, we'll help you choose the right platform for your community by walking you through a list of questions that will help you decide what works best for your setup, as well as how to utilize your existing distribution channels.

Key takeaways

- Your vision is the impact you want to see in the long term, whereas your mission is what you are doing now to work towards that.
- Your values shape the culture of your community, and the rules provide practical guidance on how to put those values into action.
- You need to be clear on your vision, mission and values from the start, although these will likely evolve over time.
- You should create a code of conduct and ensure this is clearly communicated to all members, and that they are updated on any changes.
- You should ensure that any new member agrees to abide by the rules and/or code of conduct before they join.
- There are three monetization models to choose from: free, freemium and paid, and choosing a model that involves fees requires careful consideration.

Reflection questions

Now it's time to set your vision and mission! Use these questions to guide you.

1 What do you want to achieve in the long term with your community, and where can you start working towards that?

2 What values are important to you as a business, and how do these relate to your community?

3 What conduct do you expect from members, and what would be unacceptable?

Notes

1 IKEA. The IKEA vision and values, no date, www.ikea.com/gb/en/this-is-ikea/about-us/the-ikea-vision-and-values-pub9aa779d0 (archived at https://perma.cc/2ER7-7557)

2 T J Law. 17 seriously inspiring mission and vision statement examples (2024), Oberlo, 10 November 2023, www.oberlo.com/blog/inspiring-mission-vision-statement-examples (archived at https://perma.cc/MNM3-RBQF)

3 Amazon. 18 April 2018, Our mission, www.aboutamazon.co.uk/news/job-creation-and-investment/our-mission (archived at https://perma.cc/YR5H-M96H)

4 Sanity. Community Code of Conduct, 2024, www.sanity.io/docs/community-code-of-conduct (archived at https://perma.cc/W66U-XGVF)

5 Women in Tech SEO. The WTS Way, 2024, www.womenintechseo.com/code-of-conduct/ (archived at https://perma.cc/P7YU-G4S5)

6 Women in Tech SEO. Community Partners, 2024, www.womenintechseo.com/partners/ (archived at https://perma.cc/V5NG-NLPA)

7 Women in Tech SEO. WTSFest, 2024, www.womenintechseo.com/conference/ (archived at https://perma.cc/U5YN-UAJ4)

Choosing your platform

3

One of the first stages in building your community is to choose the platform on which you will create it. There are a huge number of platform options, but don't feel daunted by this task. In this chapter, we will narrow down the type of space that will best meet your needs and those of your audience by looking at the different needs of online, offline and hybrid communities, and exploring some of the most popular platform options available.

I'll share insights from my own journey in selecting platforms and provide a process to help you make the best choice for where your community can live.

Finding the right platform for you

Your community may be an online community, an offline community or a hybrid of both online and offline. Right now, there are more platforms than ever, and they keep increasing every year.

Most community builders spend a reasonable amount of time in the setup, thinking about how to construct the best home. However, don't get stuck at this stage. The choice can feel overwhelming, even paralyzing – just make a choice and get going. You'll learn about your audience and your needs as you go, and you can adapt accordingly. It's okay if you change your mind down the line and choose to either add other platforms or migrate onto another platform. Make the best choice you can for now.

Here are five questions to answer when choosing the right platform for you.

1. Where does your audience live?

You know your audience more than anyone, so you already have a clear idea of where they currently spend their time. Are there platforms that are relatively familiar to them? Do they have a preference for social channels? Do they consume more text articles or video?

Some platforms are known to be famous for specific audiences. For example, when someone mentions Discord, the first audience that comes to mind is 'gamers'. If you were starting a gaming community, Discord might be a popular platform choice because a large audience already lives there.

If you're able to look at some data upfront and know, for example, that 'Most of my audience is already on LinkedIn', 'We get a lot of engagement on Facebook', or 'We're very popular on X', 'This is where we have our most followers', then this will give you a good starting point for determining where you could start that community because you have an audience already active there.

It's also worth considering stickiness. Platform stickiness means ensuring that this is a platform that's easy for people to stick to, or that they're aware of or comfortable using. If you decide to host your community on a not-so-popular third-party web tool or host it on a specific community app that requires you to download it on your phone, that might be difficult. If people aren't used to visiting these particular websites or apps daily, they might struggle to remember to visit them regularly, so it doesn't feel like a sticky platform. If, on the other hand, your chosen platform already forms a part of their routine, they're going to be in the environment frequently, making them more likely to engage with your community while they're there.

2. Is your community online, offline or hybrid?

Choosing upfront whether your community is online, offline or hybrid will help dictate which platform to go for.

Online communities live in the digital world and can easily connect people from around the world in one place. Offline communities are more location-based and rely on meeting in a physical space but are more likely to require an online element to help distribute and

Figure 3.1 Community types

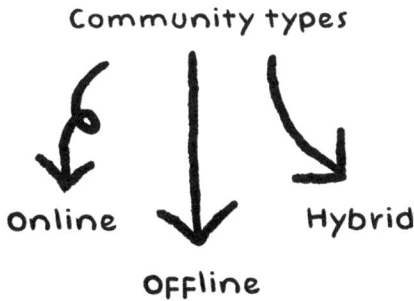

communicate their plans. A hybrid community is a mix of both, where a part of the community happens online, and a part of it happens offline through events and meetups.

In the next section, we'll dive more into different examples of each, but a big part of how your community platform will be set up is based on whether the engagement is online, offline or a mix of both.

3. How familiar are you with the platform?

As a company, if you are already set up on a specific platform, then it might make sense to use it. As a company, think about which platforms you and your team are comfortable using frequently and are most familiar with. It becomes a time drain if your team has to pull out of one platform they're using regularly to go to another with different functionality to manage this community. In addition, if you're unclear on how the platform works and what different features are available, it could lead to a clunky experience for members, and you won't be able to help them get the most from it. As someone running the community and actively using it, you should prioritize one you're comfortable with.

In my conversation with Knut Melvær, Head of Developer Community and Education at Sanity, he mentioned that his team was already set up on Slack and using it all day long in the course of their normal work, which also meant they had come to know it inside out. So, when they came to set up a community, it made sense to host it on Slack. We dive deeper into Sanity's community story in Chapter 13.

4. What features are you looking for?

Every platform has different features; you may regard some as necessary, but others not. A few things to consider:

- **Moderators:** How many moderators do you need? What user roles and content moderation options will they require?
- **Channel types:** Do you need both public and private channels? Will you control who has access to which channels? What controls will be placed on who can set them up?
- **Direct message options:** Do you want your members to interact with one another via direct message? If so, would this only be 1:1 or also in a group setting?
- **File sharing:** Is file-sharing essential for you, and is there a requirement for size or storage capacity?
- **Audio and video content:** Do you want your community to only share text content, or do you want them to be able to share audio, video and/or other media?
- **Customization:** How far can you customise your branding and other elements of the platform?
- **Historical data:** What storage capacity do you need for historical data? How long do you need to retain access to it?
- **Analytics:** What insights do you need to be able to view? What data per member and channel do you need access to?

5. What is your budget?

There's no denying it: budget is likely one of the most important factors when choosing your platform. Platform costs might include a one-off or subscription plan, a setup fee or any customization charges.

Starting a community is a long-term commitment, and it will require a dedicated budget and resources, with your tech and platform setup being one of them. For that reason, it's essential to do your research upfront and gain an understanding of how much it would cost for you to maintain your platform.

Some platforms have different costs for different sizes of community, so consider whether your chosen platform will be sustainable as you scale.

Online platforms

There are a large number of platforms that can be used and set up for your online community. I'll dive into a few that I have personal experience with.

Facebook groups

Facebook groups are very popular because they've been around the longest now. The main advantage of a Facebook group is that many people are already on Facebook, so it quickly ticks two points we mentioned above:

- Where does your audience live?
- How familiar are you with the platform?

It's straightforward for people to join groups on Facebook because they already use it daily on a personal basis. But one potential major disadvantage is that it might feel like you are crossing that line or boundary between personal and professional. There is something about a Facebook group that may feel too intimate. Many people may be used to being part of Facebook groups linked to their local neighbourhood groups, family and friends, or shared interest groups, as opposed to professional groups.

LinkedIn groups

LinkedIn groups are the complete opposite of Facebook groups. Most people use LinkedIn for their careers, so LinkedIn groups feel more professional. It also helps tick the same two points as Facebook groups, with where your audience lives and how familiar you are with the platform, because many people use LinkedIn daily.

Slack

Slack is predominantly known as a work platform for companies, but lately, many communities use it as their primary platform.

The reason is it ticks off the familiarity point. It's straightforward for brands to create another workspace dedicated to their community. With many people already using Slack in their day-to-day work, if you have different workspaces connected, you can easily tap from one to the other without having to switch to another platform.

Discord

As mentioned earlier, Discord is popular with the gaming community but has also been gaining traction with other communities. It is designed as a community platform, facilitating instant messaging via chat as well as voice calls and video calls.

Discord is the community platform of choice for Buffer, and we'll explore how they've made use of this platform in Chapter 14.

WhatsApp communities

WhatsApp communities are gaining popularity in recent years. They rely on user familiarity. Admins can create a community on WhatsApp to bring members together in topic-based groups. I'm personally a member of a number of WhatsApp communities, and I find them very intuitive to use and be a part of.

Other platforms

There are many more platforms, such as Khoros, Circle and Mighty Networks. I touched on the ones that I have personal experience with, both as a community builder and member. It's important to take your time researching the ones that work best for you, and trialling a few out before you settle on one.

Offline platforms

Many communities are built to connect their members offline through in-person meetups and conferences, whether in a single location or several locations.

Whether those are run for free or ticketed, or otherwise monetized through sponsorship or partnership, running offline events can be expensive with the cost of venue hire fees, catering and more. We dive into connecting your members through events and how to go about setting that up in Chapter 6.

As a company, if you already have established offices somewhere, then a cost-effective option might be to always host your meetups at your headquarters. Or you could collaborate with partners that have office space you can use. If not, then you will easily find a large number of different venues available in your local area.

INBOUND by HubSpot is a famous example of a community-led event. Christina Garnett, fractional chief customer officer and advisor, describes it as: 'It's all about the people. You can go to INBOUND and never hear anything about HubSpot; that's how non-salesy it is. Instead, it focuses on celebrating everyone in the community.'

Online facilitation tools

Even if a community is primarily offline, most comms will be online. Whether through email, social media channels or an attendee group, there will be the need to set up online facilitation tools that help connect attendees and keep them informed about upcoming offline events.

Two that are particularly popular are Meetup and Eventbrite.

Meetup

Meetup.com is a website designed to enable event organizers and attendees to connect. Organizers can set up their groups and share details on the different meetup events they plan to hold. Members can join these groups, RSVP to the events and browse different meetups based on location and interest.

Eventbrite

Eventbrite is an all-in-one ticketing and discovery platform. It is used by a large number of event organizers looking for a reasonably straightforward way to set up their events, make them visible for easy discovery from potential attendees and get RSVPs.

Hybrid platforms

Your typical everyday community tends to have a combination of both online and offline, making it a hybrid community. Depending on your goal and purpose, there may be more emphasis on either online or offline.

Here are a few examples of platforms that can be used to facilitate hybrid communities.

Zoom

Zoom is a communication platform that allows users to connect with audio, video and chat. It became more popular during the pandemic.

It's famous for hosting online meetups, webinars and workshops. With options for virtual meetings, team chat, online whiteboards and events, there's something for everyone, and it's familiar to many who use it for work.

Google Meet

Google Meet quickly ticks off the familiarity aspect, with many people already familiar with the Google Workspace suite and using it regularly in their day to day. It can be used for smaller group conversations or more extensive webinars and can be either free or require a subscription fee depending on your setup.

Your distribution channels

Before you begin to set up your community, you will most likely already have a distribution channel ecosystem, which consists of your website, email newsletter, social media channels and any other plat-forms that you use to communicate with your audience.

These existing channels can be leveraged to help build your community and may form the basis for it initially. For example, you may begin by increasing your email subscribers and encouraging engage-ment on that platform or generating a high volume of discussion on X (formerly known as Twitter), before migrating over to Slack or using that online conversation to point to events on Meetup.

Whether your community is open or closed, your website is an integral part of your distribution as it's the most public-facing part of your community. Brands may choose to have a landing page ded-icated to people to learn more about their community. For inde-pendent communities, these are likely hosted on a dedicated website domain.

If your website is your first point of introduction of your commu-nity to your audience, then ensure that all the relevant information is added there. Providing details on the join process, how the commu-nity is set up, and the code of conduct and who this community is for helps answer questions in advance and motivates people to join be-cause your prospective members will have all the answers they need upfront.

In the next chapter, we talk more about ways to leverage your ex-isting channels to help spread the word about your community.

You should set up your distribution channels in a way where they all work together collaboratively, providing different things to your audience depending on their needs in that space and the functionality of the particular platform, but all working towards your overall com-munication goals.

My journey with community platforms

With my community, Women in Tech SEO (WTS), my initial idea was a monthly meetup in London, because this is where I was based, for our community members to come together. The first thing I created was a page on Meetup.com, before I even created our online group.

After a few days of sharing that on social media, it was obvious that many people were interested in it, and many people joined the Meetup.com group. There is no option to have conversations within a Meetup.com group, because it's more focused on the creation of offline events, but I wanted the people who would be coming to my group to be able to talk to each other. So, within two or three days, I put together a Facebook group for WTS. It immediately became apparent from the people joining that interest wasn't limited to just London, or even the UK.

Why did I go with Facebook? The honest answer is that I was used to using Facebook groups. I had yet to join or come across LinkedIn groups myself. In retrospect, I would have created it as a LinkedIn group, as it was a lot more professional. But I made a Facebook group because I was already active there, and it was effortless and straightforward to set up a group in that space. It's free, and there are a lot of options for moderation. There isn't a limit to how many people can join. It's straightforward for people to post and comment back to one another.

Distribution-wise, I shared that this group has been created on my own personal social media accounts. Then, a few months later, I posted a poll on the Facebook group and asked people how they would feel about a Slack group. I had come to realize that a large proportion of my target audience weren't active on Facebook and/or didn't want to be part of a Facebook group, whereas they were active on Slack. A lot of people responded positively to the poll, so I set up our Slack workspace.

We continued in this way for a full year, as a hybrid community with online discussion and offline meetups. Then, in 2020, we hosted our first in-person full-day conference. This worked similarly to our meetups, but on a much bigger scale. It was very well-received, and we were planning more such events. Until the pandemic happened.

In March 2020, I realized we would have to stop all in-person events for the foreseeable future. What should we do now? Much emphasis went back to the Facebook and Slack groups, as these were already active and engaged. Then in June of that year, we launched online webinars and workshops. Initially, this was done using Zoom Pro. Afterwards, we migrated to Zoom Webinars because it gave us far more customization options.

In 2022, we resumed our offline events again, in the form of full-day conferences, and expanded our locations over the years.

To this day, we still have both the Facebook and Slack groups, which are very active, with a little over 10,000 members in total as of September 2024. Of course, we have some overlap between membership across platforms, but a fairly high proportion of members are only on either Facebook or Slack. Personally, I prefer Slack because it feels a lot more professional. I also very much appreciate the way different channels can be set up for different topics, and conversations can be categorized naturally. It makes it much easier for people to find areas of interest or locate particular conversations they want to be part of based on the channel.

For example, we have a channel around technical SEO, one around digital PR and also around analytics. Then we also have some soft-skill channels. We have channels around career and channels around motivation. We also have things like a jobs channel, where we share job opportunities, and a freelance channel, where we share freelance opportunities. We have one for opportunities where we share calls for speakers, writer pitches and things along those lines. Then we have a main announcement channel, where any new updates related to the community, new initiatives or anything like this can be shared.

With Slack, there's a lot of moderation in place, which you have a high degree of control over. Moderation tools include the ability to delete messages if needed. Like Facebook, you can remove members or make sure members don't join again.

Figure 3.2 The WTS community platform timeline

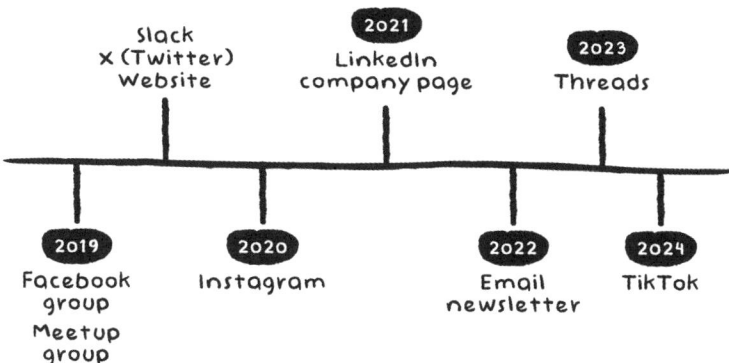

If I reflect on our journey with platforms over the past five years, it would look something like Figure 3.2.

As of 2024, these are the everyday platforms that we use:

- **Online:** Slack and Facebook Group
- **Offline:** physical hire venues and spaces
- **Hybrid:** Zoom and Google Meet
- **Distribution channels:** email newsletter and social media channels

It's okay to feel overwhelmed

Choosing a platform that's right for your community may feel overwhelming. Let's recap the initial five questions that we laid out to help you decide:

1 Where does your audience live?

2 Is your community online, offline or hybrid?

3 How familiar are you with the platform?

4 What features are you looking for?

5 What is your budget?

If you have a few platforms in mind, then a simple grid matrix where you can measure them against these five questions would be the best place to start. You'll likely end up with only one or two platforms that tick most of these boxes.

To take it a step further, you could even apply different weight scoring based on which question matters to you the most. For example, for some, it may be budget, for others, it may be familiarity.

And please remember, there is no such thing as the 'right' or the 'one' platform for a community.

As you grow and scale, you may decide to make changes; you may also have different platforms set up for different purposes. Nothing is permanent, and it's okay if you don't end up sticking to the platform that you initially decided on.

The community space is booming, and new solutions are continually being built to better serve community builders and leaders, so always be on the lookout for new possibilities that might be more relevant to your audience's needs.

What comes next

We've now come to the end of our first section, where we covered the steps for launching your community. We started with finding your why to ensure a clear purpose and direction. We then discussed the importance of defining your culture through your vision, mission, values and code of conduct. Finally, in this chapter, we talked about choosing the right platform for your community, ensuring that it aligns with the needs of your members.

In the next section, we'll explore growing your community, starting with the first steps to take to spread the word and bring people in through the door.

Key takeaways

- Your choice of platform doesn't have to be forever – don't be overwhelmed by the number of options, just choose one that will work for your needs right now, and feel free to make changes as your community evolves.

- Choosing a platform that both your audience and your internal team are already familiar with and use regularly will make it much easier to drive engagement.

- You need to consider the specific features you require, and how you want your community to work in practice.

- There are a number of different platforms that can support you in building a community online, offline or using a hybrid model.

- Leverage your existing distribution channels to build and grow your community.

Reflection questions

Now that you're ready to choose your platform, use these questions to guide you.

1 What do you imagine taking place within your community on an average day? What interactions and connections need to be facilitated? What moderation might be required?

2 What platforms are you familiar with? Which do you love and which do you really not enjoy using? Why?

3 Who are your audience? Where do they spend their time? What platforms are they active on in the course of their day-to-day lives?

PART TWO
Growing your community

Spreading the word

4

Launching your community is only the first step; growing it is what comes next.

As community builders, there's a lot of unlearning we'll need to go through before we start this new phase. We may approach growing our communities from the perspective of a marketing manager, and attempt to tie everything back to metrics that are all quantitative in nature.

My advice for you is to approach community growth with a focus on building trust between you and your members. Community is all about fostering human connections, and you can't always measure that in numbers.

Growing your membership takes time and effort, but it also gains momentum over time. Those first few people through the door are the hardest to attract, but they can be incredibly valuable for laying the foundations and easing your way to future expansion.

The focus on quality

One common mistake that new community builders make is to focus on the numbers. It's easy to fall into the trap of defining success by how many new sign-ups you get in the first month, first three months or first six months. Numbers, however, are meaningless without engagement.

The mark of a truly successful community is the quality of the conversations that are happening in the group.

Figure 4.1 Quality over quantity

Quality > Quantity

You could have 10,000 new members join your community in the first month, but, if they sit on a virtual platform silently and never interact, then they're adding no value to your community or to your business. In fact, the lack of activity might be off-putting, and could potentially stop members of your ideal audience from joining, so this vast number of members might end up being detrimental.

On the other hand, if only 10 new members join in that first month but they are highly engaged, they create meaningful interactions and build a strong relationship with you, which might then lead them to become customers and could help attract future members, then you are now in a stronger position than if you had those 10,000 unengaged members.

Shifting your mindset to seeing quality engagement as the primary goal in the preliminary stages of building your community will help ensure that you attract the right people and leverage them effectively in these crucial early days.

Leveraging existing channels

So how do you get those first few quality members? One of the best places to start is your existing channels. This might be your social media, your website, a newsletter, other online or in-person groups, and any other existing distribution mechanisms.

If you already have an engaged audience elsewhere, these are people who are primed to be invited into a closer relationship with you. Sharing with them that you have a community, and explaining how they would benefit from joining, should be a priority for your initial promotion.

Think about how you can use your channels to draw attention to your community, both with the content you share on those channels and in the mechanism of the channel itself. For example, could your email newsletter include a link to your community in the footer? Can you add a sign-up button to the header of your website? How about a sign with a QR code displayed at events?

REAL-WORLD EXAMPLE Expert insights

At The TEFL Org, Alan Moir, operations manager and community leader, told me that they have been considering this very question of how their existing channels can work harder to signpost people to their community. For example, interesting discussions are often sparked during webinars, but these conversations and the information shared will be lost once the webinar ends if there is nowhere else for attendees to take it. So, directing them to the community provides an opportunity to continue the discussion and maintain the engagement.

Alan also notes that the placement of messaging is a key consideration. If a link to the community is at the bottom of an email that contains other important calls to action, for example, it can easily be lost: 'In [a course welcome] email, people are really excited to get in and on with the course, but they might not read the whole email.' We dive deeper into The TEFL Org's community story in Chapter 12.

At HubSpot, Christina Garnett told me that they have a number of touchpoints where people are prompted to join the community. When someone begins a course with HubSpot Academy, they are invited to join a study group within the community. When a user comes to the Support team with a question, they are encouraged to connect with similar users in the community to further develop their understanding. They also create spaces for people with particular niche interests, or who have attended HubSpot events, or who want to connect to others with common elements of identity in their industry.

The process to find and join your community should be as simple and seamless as possible – if it becomes too complicated, users will simply give up. Therefore, considering elements such as the positioning of links on your website or other channels, and how you display them (e.g. through the use of buttons), is an important step not to be overlooked.

At Sanity, Knut Melvær told me that, when they first launched their community on Slack, they were keen to make sure calls to action were everywhere encouraging people to join. There were prominent links on their website and documentation, but the process was still a little clunky. 'You had to do this weird thing to let people self-join Slack. You had to set up websites and talk to the API, then send an invite because of Slack restrictions,' Knut says. 'Then we realized that, "Hey, we can just automate this!" So, every time someone signs up for a new account, we just send them the Slack invite.' Now every new customer who signs up for a Sanity plan (paid or free) is automatically invited to the community, which means most end up joining. 'That has probably played a big part in how we were able to grow it,' Knut says.

Creating a relationship between your existing channels and your community also helps to drive visibility and demand. For example, discussions or questions shared in your community could be used to create social media content, or you could share snippets or teasers of content that can be viewed in full by joining the community.

The right time and place

Another important consideration is at what point in their interactions with these channels that you want people to become aware of your community. This will come back to the purpose of your community that we discussed in Chapter 1.

If your community is for everyone, and particularly if it is part of your process to attract and nurture potential new customers, then you want people to become aware of it as quickly as possible. You will want mentions of your community, and links to access it, to be prominent, and you will share them frequently.

However, you might want people to join your community after they have had a chance to understand your brand in more depth, and/or to have begun to build a relationship with you. Perhaps you want to invite people to join your community as part of the sign-up process for your newsletter, or after they've opened a certain number of emails from that newsletter. Or you may want to suggest that someone joins your community as the next step after they have begun a free trial of your product.

Then again, perhaps you are building a community that is exclusively for your super users, in which case you will want to be far more selective about who you invite into this space.

Both Sanity and HubSpot decided against this approach, though, and Knut and Christina both advise involving free users as well to strengthen the engagement and value that the community can offer. 'If it's a place where you're only allowed to be here if you're a certain paid user, that's a country club. That's not community,' Christina says.

Knut says that Sanity's goal was to create a community for developers first and foremost, and that means all users are welcome. 'Everyone, if you're an enterprise [paid] or free member, is part of the community, and that is what's happening. There are quite a lot of enterprise developers who are in our support channels, but they are also participating in the community, helping out, or asking questions there for their private projects. There's no hard line between this.'

Allowing all users to be part of the community fits with HubSpot's ethos and values, and Christina says that the knowledge that these users can share benefits everyone. 'There are people in the HubSpot community who are in our ecosystem who are not paid users. That's fine. That's not a bug, that's a feature. That creates an opportunity for them to be a part of the community. It's really important to be able to do that.'

The purpose of your community and your intended audience will influence the channels that you use to promote it, the messaging you use to talk about your community, and the positioning of that messaging within your channels and your customer journey.

Onboarding

Once someone takes the step from one of your existing channels into your community, the initial experience is crucial. The onboarding process needs to guide them carefully so they can find their way around and use the platform with ease. If a new user is confused, overwhelmed or simply fails to see the community's benefit to them straight away, there's a good chance they may leave and never return.

Some mechanisms that can support a smooth onboarding include:

- A checklist for a new member to complete to take them through the setup process and the different features of the community.

- Automatically generated messages that introduce new members to different features and encourage them to take certain actions over a period of time (e.g. one message a day for the first week).

- Introduction posts to welcome new members and introduce them to the community.

- Follow-up emails or messages to check in with new members, asking how they're getting on and addressing any questions or concerns they have (this not only gives you a chance to encourage engagement with the platform but also provides you with useful feedback on how you can improve the onboarding process in future).

How we onboard our members at WTS

Our members join our community by filling out a form that is embedded on our website Join page.

We keep the form simple, asking for full name, email, role, company, location, LinkedIn URL and a free-form question on how they heard about our community. More importantly, we have a few checkmarks, one of which is mandatory – an agreement to abide by our terms and conditions – and our code of conduct. The others are optional on subscribing to our newsletter and if their company would like to know more about ways to partner with our community.

We add a note that invites are sent out once a week; it's important to set that expectation from the forefront, as it can feel frustrating for someone to fill out a form and feel unsure about what the next steps are.

When a new member is added to our Slack community workspace, they receive an email notifying them, and once they access our community space, an automated message is sent via direct message to welcome them. This message is sent from a welcome bot and is set up using the Automation tools on Slack. Transparency is key in ensuring that people understand this is an automated message. Here's an example of our WTS welcome message to new members.

Hey,

We're so pleased that you've joined the WTS community.

We are a free global community in search, marketing and tech. Our engaged members come from all walks of life. Together, we are changing the industry. One conversation at a time. We welcome all people of marginalized genders.

Our community has over 10,000 members across our Slack and Facebook groups. You can also connect with us on LinkedIn, X, Threads and Instagram. We also host WTSFest, our international global conference, all around the world – you can find out more about it here: London, Berlin, Philadelphia, Portland and Melbourne.

You can learn about all our different initiatives on our website, subscribe to our newsletter, and you can support us by buying us a coffee.

In order to maintain a safe and supportive group, please familiarize yourself with The WTS Way, our code of conduct.

Amplify Yourself

Here are some ways the WTS community can help you amplify yourself:

1 If you're a speaker or interested in becoming one, you can add your speaker profile and join brilliant speakers on our Speaker Hub.
2 If you're a founder, you can add your founder profile and join brilliant founders on our Founder Hub. Simply fill the form on our hub.
3 You can share your SEO story with us through our weekly WTSInterview initiative and join brilliant industry folks who already shared their stories. Simply fill the form linked in each interview piece.
4 If you're a freelancer, you can add yourself to our Freelancers/ Consultants List. Simply follow the instructions in the sheet.
5 Our weekly WTSNewsletter brings subscribers the latest news from those in the SEO industry. You can fill out a form linked on the page that includes your recent pieces to be featured in our newsletter.

To Help You Around Slack

1 Please intro yourself in the #introductions channel if you haven't done so already, and welcome new members!

2 Main community announcements are shared in this channel #announcements

3 SEO & Digital: #digital-ai, #digital-analytics, #seo-content, #digital-pr, #seo-local, #seo-technical, #general-resources, #digital-paid

4 Industry-based: #path-agency, #path-inhouse, #path-freelance

5 Events: #general-events, #wts-meetups

6 Support: #wts-amplify-me, #general-career, #wts-jobs #wts-thanks #wts-opportunities

Please reach out to Areej AbuAli if you have any questions.

Thank you again for joining us, we're so excited you're part of our community!

All the resources mentioned in this welcome message are linked to their relevant webpages; for example, we link to our code of conduct, and our various initiatives, for people to easily access them. We regularly revisit this automated message for updates, if we make changes to our initiatives or channels, to ensure that new members don't receive outdated information.

Following that, every Monday morning, I personally share a welcome message in our Introductions channel, welcoming all the new members who joined us in the past week by tagging them in a post, and encouraging our current members to give them a warm welcome.

Here's an example of what this message looks like in our WTS space.

Everyone, please join me in welcoming our latest WTS members who joined over the past week.

Here are three things you can do to help you settle in:

1 Introduce yourself on this channel

2 Familiarize yourself with The WTS Way, our code of conduct

3 Update your Slack profile with your Full Name & Picture

Do reach out if you have any questions.

This helps achieve a nice balance of an automated welcome, and a personable welcome.

Here are two more things that can help onboard new members:

- Sending a one-week check-in direct message asking how new members are finding the space
- Sending a one-month reminder message of some of the community's initiatives and events

These can either be automated or manual, as long as any replies received are handled in a timely and personable manner.

The first conversations

In the early days of your community, the blank space can feel intimidating. You may feel that you're speaking into a void, and that you're doing most of the work in the initial conversations. Don't worry, that's entirely normal at first. If you persevere in stimulating discussions, the community will build momentum over time.

Building a community is about building relationships. Getting to know new members when they first sign up allows you to understand what they are looking for from you so that you can offer them value, and help them to feel seen and appreciated. Early introductions also allow members to build relationships with one another and strengthen the impact of the community.

Encouraging new members to introduce themselves and to share what they're looking for in this space is a great way to spark initial conversations and begin to kindle engagement, as well as a sense of connection and belonging.

Other ways of generating initial engagement include:

- Polls
- Open-ended questions
- Quick one-worded response questions

Don't be alarmed, though, if you manage to generate an initial flurry of discussion, and then things quieten down. As Alan Moir at The TEFL Org points out, peaks and troughs are to be expected: 'There's a natural ebb and flow to it. Some weeks or some months, it'll be really popular and engaged, and then there'll be dips.'

This is particularly common in the early days, when new members have come into the community full of excitement and energy, and then, over time, this starts to quiet down – perhaps their initial enthusiasm has settled into a more passive, receptive mode, or maybe they've got what they needed from the community already. Alan has observed this in action: 'There'll be people that'll be really engaged because at that time that was what their goal was, or that's what they were looking for, or that's what they were needing. Then, they'll naturally maybe grow out of it, or it might not be as relevant to them now as it was maybe six months ago.'

It can be stressful when engagement drops, but if you maintain the work you've been doing to drive conversations and attract new members, you'll see it rise again. New members come with their own excitement and needs to start the cycle again, and they also reinvigorate older members who suddenly find themselves in a position to offer help, guidance and support to people who are in a similar situation to where they were at the beginning of their own journey.

Your long-term aim is to create a space where you are no longer needed – or, at least, where you are needed less. You want your community to become largely driven by the members, and building opportunities for them to connect to and support one another is what will enable your community to build meaningful momentum.

At HubSpot, although they have an incredible Support team on hand to answer questions, Christina says the community offers an extra layer of support and guidance from peers using the platform in a similar way. 'You can always go to Support if you have questions, but also, if you just have general questions or you want to see how other people are using the tool, you can join the community, and you can ask people. It's never, "Use them, not us"; it's very much, "This is a great supplement for you to connect with other people, see how they're using the tool". Maybe you have a similar use case, and you just need to talk it over with somebody to be like, "Has anyone ever used it in this capacity? What did you do, because I'm not sure how to get started?" Things like that.'

Similarly, Alan says that one of the major attractions of The TEFL Org community is the vast amount of information that exists within it, only some of which is provided by the staff. 'It is a really good font of knowledge. Even though we are the training provider, there's not one golden answer to everything. When you ask in the community, you can see all the different types of responses and people's different views. We might not be the experts in a particular area, but other people in that group are, so they might have specific information about teaching in China or teaching in Japan, cultural sensitivity, and the latest information on things like applying for your visa or your work permit. You can go online, you can read it in forums, but someone that's recently gone through that can say, "This has changed now, you need to do this". It's just a lot easier for people as well – it's out with those 9–5, Monday–Friday office hours, they just get that support from other people that are in a similar position to them.'

Testimonials

Once people are on board and enjoying your community, gathering testimonials is hugely helpful in attracting further members.

Testimonials offer 'social proof' that tells your target audience that people like them are enjoying your community and finding value in it. They also create a sense that something is happening that people want to be part of. These can be displayed on your website, or more specifically, if you have a dedicated landing page for your community, to encourage people to join. They can also be shared on your social media accounts, as a way to help market your community.

You can also encourage, or even incentivize, your members to share the community on their own channels. Once community members begin to speak on your behalf, not only do they take some of the work of marketing the platform off your shoulders, but their words are likely to be viewed as more authentic; after all, your audience knows that you will say good things about your community, it's in your interests to do so, but if their peers are saying good things independently then they feel more inclined to pay attention.

This comes back to the power of a community being driven forward by its members. One of the elements that has helped strengthen the HubSpot community is the space they have created to allow members to connect to something deeply meaningful to them – a shared passion, for example, or a shared sense of identity. As a community grows, the intimacy of these early conversations can be lost and the benefits you saw from those initial interactions and introductions are eroded as the platform begins to become overwhelming, but niche communities within your community recapture that sense of closeness.

Christina explains, 'Then you feel even deeper connectivity, because when communities are so large – the HubSpot community is crazy big – that can be a drawback because it's too much going on. I want a couple of people talking to me, not a thousand. Those communities of practice underneath that give you the power of the big, but you also get the specificity of the small.'

Spreading the word for my community

When I first launched Women in Tech SEO (WTS), the initial conversations were largely driven by me. But in those early days, that opportunity to connect with the first members gave me valuable insights into what people wanted so that I could shape the community accordingly.

In the first few weeks, when we had no more than 100 members, I spent a great deal of time prompting conversations. I asked the community what kind of content they wanted to see, what discussions they wanted to be part of, what activities they would like us to organize and what initiatives they would benefit from.

Running polls and surveys on these topics helped to drive discussion, and it built excitement for what might be possible in the future. This also encouraged members to tell friends and colleagues about the community, as they wanted other people to have access to what we were creating.

Word of mouth was the main driver to bringing more members through the door for our community. Until this day, many people who join WTS mention in the join form that they heard about it from their friends, colleagues or managers. This is a level of trust that takes time to grow, for someone to organically recommend your community to others, because they feel it may benefit others.

Having a smaller number of members enabled me to connect more easily with people on a one-to-one basis, building those important personal relationships and gathering useful feedback. These personal conversations also helped to prompt people to share the community with their networks, as they felt more closely involved in driving the platform forward.

When someone joins a new community, they are excited about the possibilities and the expectations that led them there. If you can harness and channel that excitement effectively, then you will not only have an active member who helps generate engagement within your community, but you will also have someone who is promoting and championing the community externally on your behalf.

Nowadays, I put more conscious effort into encouraging our members to help us spread the word. If we're running a new initiative, I share branded visuals and ask for support amplifying them on their social channels. When some of our members take part in free training or courses that are organized by us, we ask them to help spread the word.

It took me some time to become comfortable with asking our members for help. I regularly remind our members that communities are all about giving and taking. A community's livelihood is dependent on its members giving and taking. And by having an active role in spreading the word about us, this is their way of giving back, and ensuring the sustainability of our community.

In the next chapter, we'll look at how you can retain your members and ensure that they remain engaged in your community.

Key takeaways

- Focus on the quality of conversations rather than the quantity of members in the initial stages of building your community.
- Leverage your existing channels to make joining your community as desirable and easy as possible.

- Consider at what point in the customer journey you want people to become aware of your community.

- Your onboarding process is critical to encouraging engagement and building a relationship with your new member.

- You will need to prompt engagement in the early days of your community, which also gives you a chance to learn more about what your members want from you.

- Gather testimonials as social proof to demonstrate the value of your community to other potential members, and encourage your members to share the community with their own networks.

Reflection questions

How will you get those first members into your community? These questions will help you consider your initial action plan.

1 At what point in the customer journey do you want your audience to become aware of your community?

2 What touchpoints do you have with your audience that could signpost them to your community?

3 How can you welcome new members into your community and help them to participate?

Retaining your members 5

Now that you've got your first members through the door and you have built up a strong level of engagement, you're probably thinking it's time to focus on attracting more members. Not so fast. Before you can grow your community, you need to make sure that the people who join are going to want to stick around.

The Digital Community Leaders Survey Report[1] surveyed community leaders on how they support their members, and some of the most popular responses included recognizing member contributions, replying promptly to member queries, featuring their content, providing great content and an invitation to get them involved and give them a role.

In this chapter, we'll look at some of the above tactics and understand how you can maintain long-term relationships with your members so that, when you do begin to grow, you'll be doing so in a more stable way.

Retention over growth

Right now, you're keen to grow your community, and you're probably eager to hear about approaches for marketing your platform and encouraging new visitors. But you won't achieve true growth simply by adding more people, as counterintuitive as that might sound.

One of the biggest issues that plague membership groups, subscription platforms and communities of any kind is that they lose older members as fast as they attract new ones. You can't achieve sustainable growth without retaining the members you already have. Until you have a solid retention strategy, bringing in new people is just like pouring water into a leaking bucket.

As Laura Roth points out, getting your community right at the very beginning, for your initial members, will give you a solid foundation for the future: 'I always think build the value, and they'll come, and build the value for the small set of people. It doesn't matter if you're building value for five people, because you have to start somewhere.'

It's easy to focus your goals for your community on membership growth, looking purely at numbers added. But a successful, sustainable community also focuses on retention and engagement goals, tracking metrics such as retention rate, length of membership, number of active members, number of conversations happening and so on. Laura Roth puts it beautifully: 'I'd rather have 100 very engaged people than 1,000 non-engaged people. It just doesn't do anything, but I think it's hard to get companies and brands to realize that. At the end of the day, it's not really showing any value if they've just signed up to a community and never come back to it.'

A customer who is embedded within a community will find it a lot harder and be a lot more unwilling to walk away from the brand or product that facilitates that community, because they lose so much more than just the product when they do. Christina Garnett says this has had a highly beneficial impact on the HubSpot community – the relationships people build within that space, and the resources, support and conversations they have access to, make HubSpot as a product far more valuable to customers than the functionality by itself.

For Women in Tech SEO (WTS), I can pinpoint the exact moment where I felt that we had moved on from simply bringing new members through the door to retaining them. It was when I no longer felt the need to be the main person who goes in and answers all the questions. By the time I went in, the questions were already answered by other members, and it wasn't just questions, it was also welcoming new people through the door, helping amplify one another and, even at some points, reminding members of our code of conduct. That was the point where it truly felt like our community was officially in the next stage.

Asking for feedback

Quantitative and qualitative feedback are hugely beneficial in helping you to retain members. By understanding what's working and what's not, and what your members would most value from you, you can adapt to best serve their needs and improve their experience.

This doesn't necessarily mean asking for feedback on the community as a whole – you can do that, too, and you might benefit from doing so every so often, perhaps with an annual or six-monthly community survey to capture members' overall experience. On an ongoing basis, however, you'll likely find it useful to capture more focused and regular feedback on specific elements. For example, every time you run a webinar, a workshop, an in-person or virtual networking session, or any other initiative, you'll gain helpful insights from asking for feedback.

Feedback can be sought in a number of ways. For example, at the end of an event, you could ask members for:

- A numeric score for the whole event
- Numeric scores for two or three different elements
- One thing they enjoyed, and one thing they didn't
- A mixture of quantitative and qualitative feedback – a numeric score for the event and suggestions on what could be improved

At WTS, we have a feedback scoring system. The questions we ask always require a score out of four – this means that members can't choose a point right in the middle. We need to know whether they consider the element in question to be poor or good, and forcing them to choose a side of the fence gives us a much clearer idea of how people are feeling.

Feedback surveys also provide a great opportunity to ask about new elements that you are considering rolling out. You don't want to invest time and money in creating new initiatives, channels, mechanisms, or even migrating to a new platform, if your community won't find value in this change. So, reaching out to ask for their input can help you make the decision, and shape how you take it forward.

In the previous chapter, we looked at the value of testimonials in attracting members to your community, and feedback forms are a great place to ask if respondents would be willing to provide you with a testimonial and to give them space to do so. You may also be able to collate sentences from responses to questions such as 'What do you like most about this community?' that you can use in your marketing. Make sure you ask permission before sharing a member's words publicly if you plan to name them, though – you can add a checkbox in your form asking if the respondent is happy to be quoted in marketing materials.

Feedback forms will also provide you with vital insights into the demographics of your community, and any information about who they are that might be relevant to you, such as job role or location. If you find you have a high percentage of members in a particular city, you might consider holding an event there. If you find your community is lacking in people from a certain demographic group, you might consider whether there is more you can do to make your group feel welcoming to that group.

Examples

Annual community survey

At WTS, we send out an annual survey to capture how members are feeling about the community as a whole. We ask upfront questions such as role and job function which enables us to segment our data. Our survey includes questions such as the following.

EXAMPLE

- What compelled you to look into finding a community to be part of?
- What do you believe brought you to choose WTS?
- What were some obstacles or uncertainties that cropped up when you were choosing whether to join WTS?
- What can we do to make this community a better community for you?
- What are your favourite WTS initiatives?
- What other initiatives would you like to see?
- What have you gained from joining WTS?

Initiative feedback

We also ask for specific feedback about our Slack channels. In this form, we ask questions such as the following.

EXAMPLE

- How often do you use our Slack group?
- Which channels do you regularly use?
- Which channels would you like to see added?
- Which do you prefer, the Slack group or Facebook group, and why?

Post-event feedback

WTS hosts in-person conferences, WTSFest, in a number of cities around the world. Following these events, all attendees are sent a feedback form that asks questions such as the following.

EXAMPLE

- How satisfied were you with WTSFest?
- How satisfied were you with different elements of the event, in the lead-up and on the day?
- How would you rate the agenda sessions?
- How much did you feel our code of conduct, The WTS Way, was modelled well throughout the event?
- How much did the event help you expand your professional network in a meaningful way?
- What did you like best about WTSFest?
- What could we do to improve WTSFest?
- How likely are you to attend WTSFest again?

We talk more about events and event feedback in the next chapter.

As you can see, all of these surveys include a mixture of quantitative questions (asking respondents to give a rating for enjoyment or satisfaction, or to select their favourites from a list) and qualitative questions (asking for thoughts on what they enjoy or what they would like to see in future). This provides us with a mixture of numeric results that we can track over time to see changes and trends, and that give measurable indications about what's working well and needs improving, and deeper insights and thoughts from our community that might reveal issues or ideas that we hadn't even thought to ask about.

Making use of the feedback

Don't fall into the trap of simply collecting feedback and then doing nothing with it. This data provides you with important information about how you can adapt your community to better suit and retain your members. This will, in turn, help you attract more new members in the future as you better meet their needs and grow your reputation.

You should be continually comparing feedback forms to see how responses have changed, how scores have increased or decreased, and why that might be. You will also be able to see whether the demographics, location and roles of your members are changing over time, and adapt accordingly.

Feedback can be crucial to addressing issues that might otherwise cause your community to lose members and shaping your community to attract and retain members in the future.

At The TEFL Org, Alan Moir says feedback has helped them to respond to their members' needs in a way that makes their courses better for both existing and future students. 'You can see what the pain points are and what people are concerned about or what they're discussing right now. That's fed in a lot to what we've done to improve the courses. For example, providing guidance to help people find work once they've completed the course, signposting resources or showing what they might be able to earn teaching English online. When we look at people's concerns, it can shape what we do in the future. We can say, "We're getting a lot of questions or queries about this. We need to get a resource guide together for this or put it into a webinar."'

Community ambassadors

A popular way to keep community members engaged is to launch a community ambassador programme. Community ambassadors help drive engagement inside the group, as well as market your community and brand externally.

Several terms can be used to describe them, ambassadors only being one of them, such as advocates, influencers, contributors, super users or champions. The programme we have for WTS is called the WTS Community Heroes programme.

One of the best resources I've come across for this is Feverbee's Building Successful Superuser Programs.[2] They explain that ambassador programmes are extensions of your existing community efforts and that proper strategizing is key to success.

With ambassador programmes, the primary objective tends to be one of four:

1 Brand awareness

2 Engagement

3 Leads or referrals

4 Support

As Feverbee recommend, it's useful to start by defining one objective first, and other objectives can be considered as the programme scales.

They go on to suggest several questions that can help you define that objective upfront.

- Are you hoping to drive sales, leads or referrals?
- Are you looking for a way to increase brand awareness or amplify growth?
- Do you need to boost online engagement or support new member onboarding?
- Are too many questions going unanswered in your support channels?
- Is increased site traffic or a wider social media following important?
- Are you looking for a scalable way to launch in new places?

Once an objective is identified, it's essential to measure the success of your ambassador programme by tracking its relevant metrics. We talk more about tracking community metrics in Chapter 11.

Diversifying your initiatives

I strongly believe that one of the main reasons that my community, WTS, continues to be highly engaged and to thrive as a community is that we are continually diversifying our initiatives. When a new initiative launches or a new cohort begins for an existing initiative, we see a surge in activity.

One of our most successful initiatives is our mentorship programme, WTSMentorship, a free programme that we run twice a year where we match mentors and mentees and provide them with training and guidance throughout the cohort. This is unique to our industry and something our members told us that they needed. We have developed the programme – and continue to update and reiterate it – through input from our members, and we are continually reviewing feedback to see how we can improve. What's interesting about WTSMentorship is that every time we announce a new cohort, it brings in many new members through the door, as well as helps us retain our current members and keep them engaged.

We continue to develop new opportunities, and as a community grows, you may look at introducing meetups, conferences, festivals, training courses, a podcast, a newsletter – the options are endless. None of these are unique or original, but they are unique to your community. When they are embedded in your particular values, aligned with your individual mission, and provide a way for your members to connect around the specific area of interest that brought them together in the first place, then they will offer something that your members can't find elsewhere.

Laura Roth points out that the simple act of bringing people together can have great value these days. 'Face to face is hard these days. It's changed. A few years ago, when everyone was in the office all the time, it was a lot easier to get people together on a day after work. Now, your average person is probably going in once a week, if you have an event on a different day than when they're going in, they're just not going. That makes it that much harder, and I think we're aware of that. We always wanted to make face to face our top priority because there isn't that much of that. There are a million online communities for everything, but our focus has always been about trying to connect people on a human level, actually in front of each other, as fast as we can.'

Developing and facilitating all these initiatives is a lot of work, though. And it's important to remember that your community isn't a space that should be dominated by you – it's not a platform for you to simply broadcast your own marketing. So how much better would it be if your members could initiate and implement ideas themselves? If you can provide them with the tools, motivation and sense of empowerment to do that, then not only will they be doing a lot of the work for you in terms of offering value to your members and attracting new ones, but you'll increase the sense of belonging and connection as your members feel they're truly part of something that works for them.

At WTS, we introduced location channels to our Slack community at the direct request of members who wanted an easier way to meet other members in their area. One of the channels requested was for our German members – the fact that this channel became so active and engaged was part of the reason that we chose Berlin as a location for one of our conferences. We already had enthusiastic members there, connecting with one another and hosting their own meetups, so we knew that demand was there. This is a great example of how listening to feedback can guide future decisions.

Laura Roth says that these smaller, member-driven groups can be critical to your growth. 'It's mini communities popping up within a big community because they find that one thing that connects them. I think all brands could learn a lot from those mini communities. You've got this whole big community, especially as you scale, but it's the mini groups that are going to be the ones that will add the most value for people. Maybe it's a global thing, and then you've got mini groups within a region, or you've got mini groups of people within the same industry. That's where the connection really happens. I think it doesn't need to be always in a big open forum, it can be one-on-one; I've noticed a lot of the big value almost happens behind the scenes. It's quite hard to measure, but when you find out that a member of your community has had this incredible conversation with another member that's more powerful than anything else.'

Alan Moir has seen a similar impact at The TEFL Org, where their annual graduate survey enables them to get input on new initiatives from a highly engaged and knowledgeable group before rolling them out more widely. 'It's a really good indicator of what will work and what will not work, because they've either done the course or they're doing the course, and they'll see it as relevant to them. We can get a sense check before we push out to the wider group.'

One at a time

Diversifying, however, shouldn't mean throwing a lot of things at your members all at once. I've seen many instances where community builders have got excited and started launching numerous initiatives in parallel, only to leave their audience thoroughly confused and overwhelmed.

Remember that your members are probably members of other communities as well, and they also have their day-to-day lives where they are juggling all the many information inputs that we all deal with, from work, family, internet, social media, email, community groups and so on. It's a lot to process. It's not unlikely that your members will miss a percentage of the messages that you send out, and they will need reminding about a new initiative multiple times before they fully take in that it exists, never mind try it out and get to grips with it.

Take your time introducing something new, repeating the messaging until your members have had a chance to get familiar with it. Give them some time to get used to this new thing and feel comfortable with it.

Laura Roth shares how life can interfere with even the best-laid plans. 'I set up drop-in sessions, quite similar to "meet the experts" roundtables, with two experts on hand to answer questions. We had two of them two weeks apart. The first one was the most incredible energy you've ever seen. Probably only about 15 people – that's fine, you don't need millions. But the second one was much quieter. There were only about three people there, and the energy wasn't the same.

'You have to realize, especially when you're dealing with different community members, that life happens alongside it. There were world events impacting people that week as well. It's not always about what you're actually doing, but it can be about the timing of it as well. I think that was, in a way, a good lesson to see one go really well. I'm happy it went that way round and not the other, because if you have the first one go terribly, you're much less inclined to do it again. Now we're trying to host them monthly. You need to test and continue to try different things and check out whether there are other factors that could be harming something.'

Part of the process of introducing anything new should also involve taking the time to reflect. You should look at what has gone well with the launch and what could be improved, what engagement and buzz was driven by the launch, what's working and what's not working so well in practice now that the initiative is live, and what feedback you have received from your members. You need to take learnings from this process before you embark on another one, as this will inform how you approach the next launch.

Prioritizing your initiatives

When you are full of ideas, and receiving requests from members, it can be difficult to prioritize which initiatives to take forward. One important factor to consider is the ratio of effort to impact. Some initiatives you know will require little effort but are likely to generate significant impact. Others might require a lot of effort but are unlikely to make a huge impact.

Impact + Effort = Priority

To define impact, you need to look at your goals. For example, at WTS, some of our key goals are as follows:

1 Bring in new members

2 Retain current members

3 Bring in new partners and sponsors

4 Retain current partners and sponsors

When we have an idea for a new initiative, we calculate the likely impact by considering how many of those four it is likely to influence.

The effort is calculated by considering the time, resources and budget required.

By having both your impact and effort defined, you can calculate the level of priority using the matrix in Table 5.1.

Figure 5.1 will help you visualize it.

Table 5.1   Prioritization matrix

PRIORITY RULE	PRIORITY
If Impact = L and Effort = S	High
If Impact = L and Effort = M	High
If Impact = M and Effort = S	High
If Impact = L and Effort = L	Mid
If Impact = M and Effort = M	Mid
If Impact = S and Effort = S	Mid
If Impact = M and Effort = L	Low
If Impact = S and Effort = L	Low
If Impact = S and Effort = M	Low

Figure 5.1   Impact, Effort, Priority

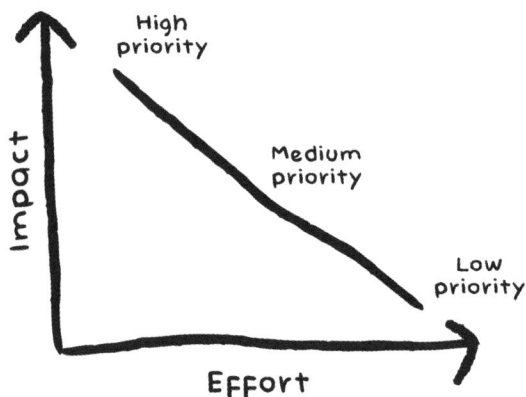

For example, if we were to apply this to two of our WTS initiatives, this is how it would look. Our mentorship programme, WTSMentorship, has a large impact and is of medium effort, which gives it a high priority. This is how we came to decide that it's worth running twice a year. On the other hand, our online workshop initiative, WTSWorkshop, has a medium impact and is of large effort, which gives it a low priority, so we don't prioritize running them over other initiatives.

Applying your own learnings

When it comes to retaining members, it can be tempting to focus solely on what they tell you they want. Feedback from your members is certainly important, but it's not the whole story. You should also take some time to reflect on what is working and not working from your point of view.

This includes assessing how much the community and its different elements are helping you meet the goals you set out at the beginning and considering whether you and your team are genuinely enjoying working on these projects.

An initiative that I put together a few years ago was WTSPodcast, our community podcast. Initially, this was something that I managed myself, but I found that I didn't enjoy working on it. I outsourced the work, but it became clear that the effort required – the cost of hiring a team to work on it, and the time it took to put each episode together – wasn't worth the impact, as it was only attracting low numbers of new members and wasn't driving much engagement. So, the podcast had to go.

I don't look back at this and think of it as a failure. I used the time, money and resources that I utilized on the podcast to focus on initiatives that have a greater impact on our members and are more enjoyable for me and the team to work on.

In the next chapter, we'll explore how events can help grow your community by building connections between you and your members. We'll discuss why events are powerful, the types you can create and the factors that help make them a success.

Key takeaways

- Focus on retention over growth.
- Regularly ask your members for qualitative and quantitative feedback on the community as a whole and on individual elements.
- Keep reviewing and analysing this feedback and use the learnings to adapt your community to better serve your members.
- Diversify your initiatives… but take it one at a time so as not to overwhelm or confuse your members.
- Prioritize initiatives by assessing the cost/impact ratio.
- Take time on a regular basis to reflect on what is and isn't working from your point of view.

Reflection questions

As you consider how to scale your community, use these questions to help you plan your approach.

1 How can you gather feedback and insights from your community on a regular basis?
2 How will you analyse and reflect on these insights?
3 What new initiatives can you offer your community, and how will you stagger these?

Notes

1 Digital Community Leaders. 2023 Digital Community Leaders Survey Report, 2023, https://digitalcommunityleaders.com/ (archived at https://perma.cc/YQ4T-JHA8)
2 Feverbee. Building successful superuser programs, nd, www.feverbee.com/superuser/goals-and-objectives/ (archived at https://perma.cc/367W-XPCR)

Connecting through events 6

When it comes to growing your community, events are a powerful tool as they centre on the main component of community building – relationships. A big part of why a lot of people seek community and want to be part of a community is the opportunity to build their network. Creating events that enable this will help you attract and retain members of whichever type of community you are building.

In this chapter, we're going to explore why events matter to your community, and the different types of events that you can create. We'll look at the considerations that go into making a successful event, and how you can learn from each one to improve your strategy as you progress.

Why events are important

Even if your business isn't events-based and events aren't a key part of your goals for your community, events can still play a valuable role in growing and retaining your membership.

Bringing your community together

Events are a powerful way to connect your existing members with one another. As we've seen, communities are all about relationships, and a big part of why your members joined in the first place is to build those relationships. When they have the opportunity to meet face to face (in person or virtually), they are better able to get to know one another, open up discussions and connect in a meaningful way.

During an event, members get to know one another as people, which strengthens their relationships and makes them feel more real than simply chatting with a screen name and inanimate profile picture. All of this encourages them to feel more deeply embedded within the community, and, by extension, more connected to your brand as you are facilitating these relationships.

The other benefit to conversations at an event is that they take place in real-time. If you have an online community, most of the communication between your members is happening on an ad hoc basis. For example, someone logs in at a certain time in their time zone, they see a few questions or discussions, then they jump in and answer or contribute to those in their own time. Then other people do the same in their own time, and so on and so forth. It isn't a continuous conversation, and it isn't a natural way to interact. At an event, however, everyone is connecting live – at the same time. Whether that connection takes place online or offline doesn't matter; all attendees have the sense of being in the same place, taking part in the same thing, and they engage in conversations in which they are present and listening to one another, responding directly to the other person. This not only fosters stronger relationships, it also encourages a greater depth of discussion.

Raising awareness of your community

As well as supporting your existing community and nurturing that all-important member retention, events can also help your community to grow. When you hold an event, you open up opportunities for new people to discover your community through different channels.

People find out about events in their area and their specific areas of interest in a range of different ways, from the venue's own promotion to local and topic lists on event pages, dedicated online groups and the networks of any partners involved in the event.

Some people may attend your event not knowing much, if anything, about your brand or community, but simply being interested in the topic. Through the event, they discover more about you, get to know existing members and are encouraged to join for themselves. This is a fantastic way to bring new people in.

Types of events to consider

There are a number of different types of events that you could host for your community, and a few considerations that will help you work out which ones are right for you.

Online or offline (or both)?

The first point to think about is whether your community is online, offline or hybrid – a combination of both.

An offline community will probably have events built into the strategy from day one, as this is most likely going to be the main method of facilitating your community. You might also consider whether you want to introduce online events to widen your reach and increase the opportunities for participation.

If you have an online community, you may start out with a platform like Slack or Discord where members can interact in their own time, and then consider adding virtual or offline events to help deepen those relationships. As mentioned above, events provide a real-time, 'face-to-face' connection that adds so much value to your community.

Offline events can range from small gatherings – perhaps an informal coffee or meal – to more structured sessions with talks and/or networking, to half-day, full-day or even multiple-day conferences. At Women in Tech SEO (WTS), when we initially started, we had in-person monthly meetups in London that took place on the first

Figure 6.1 Event types

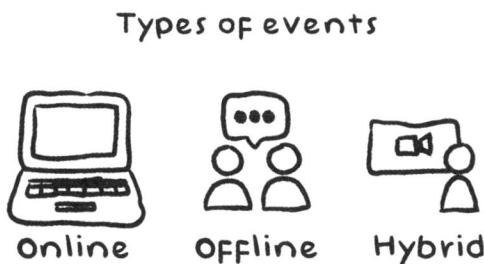

Types of events

Online   Offline   Hybrid

Wednesday evening of each month. They were a gathering of 100 people at most, where we had three short industry talks and time to network and connect with one another. Once our community grew, we started hosting WTSFest, a full-day conference that now runs in several international locations. I talk more in detail about conferences in Part 3.

Online events are likely to be shorter – asking people to sit on a video call platform like Zoom or Google Meet for extended periods of time can be draining. A virtual networking event where everyone has the opportunity to introduce themselves and talk about a specific theme, or a webinar with a speaker where participants have the opportunity to discuss the topic with one another and ask questions using the chat function usually works best. For WTS, we host regular one-hour online webinars, which we call WTSWorkshops, on Zoom that are made up of a 45-minute talk presented by a trainer, followed by 15 minutes of questions and answers.

There is also the option of hybrid events. These are events that take place in person, but have mechanisms by which attendees can join virtually. Hybrid events do involve more work than other types, because care needs to be taken to ensure that virtual attendees still have a positive experience, not simply a poor view on a badly placed webcam of a lively discussion taking place in person that they can't be part of. Having good technology, dedicated facilitators coordinating the online element of the event and putting in place mechanisms that allow everyone to contribute to the discussion are vital. For WTSFest, we offer the option of recording tickets for some of our location festivals, which gives people a chance to watch all the sessions in their own time in the comfort of their own homes.

The Digital Community Leaders Survey Report[1] recommends putting in the effort to enable a hybrid component to your event, where there is an option to access the event remotely, whether through a live stream or recordings, as these events:

- Increase accessibility and flexibility
- Extend event reach
- Provide cost savings

- Showcase innovation
- Enhance engagement and interaction
- Reduce environmental impact by decreasing travel

Let's take a look at some of the ways that you can create each category of event.

Virtual events

Types of virtual event

There are different formats that you can use for online events, including:

- **Informal discussion:** attendees are invited to have an unstructured conversation on a particular topic or theme; although the discussion is relaxed and informal, it's always good to have a host or a moderator to keep the conversation moving, deal with any issues that might arise and make sure that people keep to time.
- **Talk/workshop:** an expert speaker gives a presentation to a virtual audience, allowing attendees to ask questions and get answers; there should also be a 'chat room' or some other space where attendees can talk with one another to enable that sense of networking that is so important.
- **Community-led events:** members are able to organize their own meetups, which they plan and run themselves; for example, WTS members have created their own book club, career discussions and meetups for people who work in specific sectors. If you are going to allow your community to lead their own events, it's a good idea to provide them with guidance on how to do this effectively. This guidance should include a reminder of the community code of conduct, details on how to schedule a meeting, guidance on running a meeting and providing a post-meeting recap.

For virtual events organized by our WTS community members, we encourage them to follow five steps.

EXAMPLE

1 Introduce yourself and give a brief introduction explaining the purpose of this event.

2 Remind attendees of the community code of conduct that is to be observed throughout the event.

3 Encourage participation – with small groups, people can simply come off mute to speak, but in larger groups, utilize the functionality found in the meeting software.

4 Post-event, share a recap of the discussion, shared advice, strategies and any resources.

5 Ask for feedback to incorporate in future events.

Event requirements

Platform   When planning a virtual event, you will first need to choose a platform (if the event will take place outside the platform that you normally use to facilitate your community). We looked at some of the platforms you might consider in Chapter 3, and the same guidance applies when choosing a platform for an event as when choosing one for your community – consider what works for your audience and what functionality you need. A platform that your audience is familiar with could help to encourage engagement with the event, and you will need to think about *how* you want your audience to engage and what platforms can facilitate that (for example, do you need chat options, Q&A, polls and so on). The main platforms that we use for online events at WTS are Zoom and Google Meet.

Timing   Then, you'll need to consider the timing of your event. Make sure you let people know far enough in advance that the event will be taking place so that they can plan to attend, giving them clear information about the date and time, and how long it will run for. Check that the date you choose doesn't coincide with any major events, or religious and cultural festivals that might prevent people from being available.

If you have international members, take into account different time zones and which time zones are most common among your members. Community members may have other factors that impact what times they are available, such as whether they will be attending during working hours, and possible childcare responsibilities. You could run a poll to ask what times work best for the majority of your members. For WTS, we have found that 4pm UK time works well for the majority of our UK, EU and North American members.

RSVP   You may or may not want to provide a mechanism for people to register for the event. This can be helpful to give you an indication of numbers, or if you have a limited number of spaces, and is essential for paid events. Asking people to pre-register can also enable you to cross-check attendees with your database of community members and reduce the risk of your online event being infiltrated by non-community members. The platform that you use may have its own built-in system for this – for example, Zoom allows you to create registration links, and Google Meet can be combined with Google Calendar invites.

Accessibility   No matter how carefully you choose the date and time, some of your members will not be able to attend. Recording the session means that you can make the video available for these people to view at a later date. Make sure that everyone attending in real-time understands that the event is being recorded and that they can turn their camera off if they don't want to be visible in the recording.

Many platforms have in-built accessibility functionality that you can make use of. For example, Zoom has the option to enable live captioning. Sharing presentations and materials that will be used during the event in advance can also be helpful for some attendees. You should ask in advance of the event if attendees have any specific requirements so that you can accommodate these, such as providing sign language interpreters.

In-person gatherings   As with virtual options, you can choose to hold smaller, more informal gatherings, or more structured events. I have separated smaller meetups from large conferences, as there is a lot of thinking and planning required for the latter.

Small gatherings can be largely community-led. For example, if your community has members from all around the world, then you could give them the option to host their own local meetups. These meetups could be held in an office space or in social venues. It's a good idea to provide them with guidance on how to do this effectively. This guidance should include a reminder of the community code of conduct, details on how to schedule a meeting, guidance on running a meeting and providing a post-meeting recap.

With in-person gatherings organized by our WTS community members, we provide the following guidance for choosing a venue.

EXAMPLE

- Is the venue free to use?
- Can it hold the amount of people who are interested in the meetup?
- Is it suitable for all weather? If it is weather-dependent, do you have a plan B?
- Is it suitable for any accessibility requirements and general access?
- Is the venue safe, comfortable and conducive to conversation?
- If there is food available for guests to purchase, does it meet all dietary requirements?
- If alcoholic drinks are available, are non-alcoholic beverages as readily available?

Conferences

Conferences can take place in a single day or over the course of several days, and typically take place only once a year – although some organizations choose to host several each year, with each event taking place in a different location. At WTS, we host annual conferences in the UK, US, Germany and Australia. It's unusual for these to be community-led – most commonly there will be one business or organization that takes overall ownership of the planning and execution, potentially working with partners or sponsors that will support the process.

Location

Your first decision will be the location. Often, as a company, the simplest option is to host your conference at your business headquarters.

However, it might be worth considering where your actual members are located. If you don't hold this data already because it's not collected when new members register, then you can use a survey to find out.

When it comes to location choice, costs will also be a factor. Your own office space is free to use, whereas event venues will vary in price and may come with other logistical requirements that need to be factored into your budget.

At WTS, our annual WTSFest currently takes place in five locations around the world, with more planned for the future. This evolved gradually from our initial monthly meetups in London – when we came to hold our first full-day conference in 2020, London was the obvious choice. In 2023, we decided to expand to the US as more than 30 per cent of our members were based there, with some even travelling to London for our conference. We chose Philadelphia because we had a larger membership following based in the East Coast. Then in 2024, we introduced WTSFest Berlin to the mix – our community in Germany had been growing strongly, and we were seeing many local meetups being held in Berlin and around the country. This is a good example of how community activity can guide you in developing and planning initiatives.

In 2025, because of our growing base in North America, we plan to add another conference for the West Coast, taking place in Portland Oregon, to complement the one we already have on the East Coast in Philadelphia. Due to popular demand, we're also looking at Melbourne, Australia for late 2025. We're guided by our community and where we know there are people eager to attend these events.

Several challenges may arise when planning international conferences. This includes not having a full understanding of the market, working with international suppliers and facilitating international payments. At WTS, here are a few things we do to mitigate that from happening:

- Work with our lawyers and accountants to ensure that our planning is legally and financially compliant with these markets
- Prioritize working with local suppliers and team members, which means a better understanding of the culture and our attendees' expectations

- Work with venues that have experience working with international clients, so there are processes in place that facilitate us to do most of our planning virtually

Pricing

There are a number of costs to consider when organizing a conference. These include:

- **Venue:** the biggest cost of all, which includes the space itself, catering and audio-visual equipment. Lots of venues offer DDR (day delegate rate), which is usually an easier option.
- **Supporting events:** if you wish to hold a pre- or after party, you might require an additional venue, catering and other elements.
- **Speaker expenses:** if you are paying experts to share their knowledge with your audience, you will need to pay them, and you may also want to offer them travel and/or accommodation expenses.
- **Team expenses:** the costs of travel, food and accommodation (if necessary) for your staff.
- **Suppliers:** you will likely want a photographer and videographer to document the day, and you may want to provide activities or other elements for your audience. You may find that there are members of your community who can help you here, either by providing low-cost services or by providing their services for free in exchange for a conference ticket.
- **Logistics:** some elements to consider are stationery, name badges, lanyards, printouts and so on.

These costs might simply come from your marketing budget, if you decide that this event is purely a marketing expense. However, you might also be able to monetize the event. You could choose one or both of the following:

- **Sponsors:** find businesses that want to speak to your audience and ask them to sponsor your event in exchange for promotion and/or exhibition space at your event.
- **Paid tickets:** charge for entry to the event, with a range of different ticket options (super early bird, early bird, standard, group discounts, scholarship tickets, recording-only tickets, etc.).

Make sure that you forecast from the start so that you understand how much your event will cost and how much income you need to generate in order to break even. Then you can set expectations and targets for how many sponsors and/or ticket sales you need to generate different levels of profit. You can also plan all your costs carefully to avoid any unpleasant surprises. Having all that fleshed out from the start ensures that your conference can be financially viable.

Working with your speakers

You will want to be clear from the beginning about what topics you want to cover at your event and what your audience wants to know – you could even run polls ahead of time in your community to find out what specific topics they would most like to see covered. Then you can work closely with the speakers and trainers to ensure the talks and workshops deliver the value you and your audience were looking for.

The best way to ask for potential speakers to put themselves forward is via a 'pitch form'. These are online forms (it can be as simple as a Google Form or a form embedded on your website) that ask for details about the speaker, their topic and perhaps their experience as a speaker. This gives a fairer chance to a broader range of people, rather than simply inviting people you already know. You can then evaluate the different proposed talks and see which ones will add the most value to your community.

The more guidance you provide in a pitch form, the better. You could explain the duration of the talk, and the topic ideas you're searching for, as well as provide examples of previous successful pitches.

Speakers are important – they are the primary reason why conferences sell tickets. At the end of the day, your attendees are coming to hear those talks. So, look after your speakers. Consider what you will offer them in the way of fees, expenses and perks. At WTS, we pay all our speakers and give them a travel expense budget.

Diversity among your speaker line-up is key. At WTSFest events, we ensure at least 50 per cent of all speakers are people of colour. We connect with different communities and organizations and outreach directly to individuals to increase awareness of our speaking opportunities among underrepresented communities. We also encourage our own community members to pitch to speak to involve and empower our members.

Communication

It's important to keep all your attendees informed before, during and after the event in order to create a seamless experience.

Keep your event landing page up to date with all the latest information and send out countdown email communication three months, two months and one month before the event which remind everyone of the key details (such as timings, location, agenda, dress code, etc.) and answer any questions you've received.

Having an FAQs (frequently asked questions) document or web page is helpful, as you can bring together the main questions that you're likely to get and signpost potential attendees to these rather than responding to the same question over and over. You can add to this as you see what other questions come in regularly.

You can find an example of the WTSFest FAQs on our conference hub page.[2]

You will see that we have put the questions into categories to help people find the information they need easily. The categories we use are:

- Speakers, attendees and agenda
- Location, timings and facilities
- Ticket types and code of conduct
- Sponsors and suppliers

At WTS, we even created our own event app using evntt.io[3] to share the conference agenda, help people connect in advance, introduce themselves, chat with each other, and send announcements before and during the event day itself. If you prefer to not have a separate app for that, you can also utilize your community space, such as your Slack group or similar, to give room for your attendees to connect.

Networking

As we've discussed, a big reason why people attend events like these is because they want to network with one another. Providing opportunities throughout the event, and at supporting events, can greatly increase the appeal of your event.

Here are a few ideas for networking activities:

- **Speed networking:** this is where each attendee has a few minutes to speak to each person in the room.

- **Roundtable discussions:** opportunities for a group of attendees to sit down and discuss a particular topic, often facilitated by an expert.

- **Networking bingo:** a way to encourage people to talk to others that they don't know by giving them particular questions to ask or topics to discuss to tick off their bingo sheet.

- **Pre-conference meetup:** hosting a casual meetup the evening before your conference gives attendees a chance to meet each other in advance and helps break the ice.

- **Buddy system:** pairing up attendees with one another in advance so that they can have a buddy on the day; this is especially useful for attendees going to a conference on their own.

Meeting attendees' needs

Accessibility is key for an event, and it shouldn't be an afterthought.

It's important to ask at ticket registration if attendees have any accessibility needs that they'd like to disclose, and to have an easy way for people to get in touch with to ask about accessibility requirements.

For WTSFest, we specifically call that out in our FAQs on our conference hub page, where we include the following question: 'I have specific accessibility needs that I'd like catered for; who do I ask?', and we provide an email address to reach out to for these inquiries. We also share an Access and Welfare Guide with our attendees that includes information on getting to the venue, the venue layout, attendee facilities, assistance and emergency procedures.

Over the years, we've added several considerations to our events that have supported our attendees including providing accessible bathrooms, a parent room, a quiet space, a prayer room and baby changing facilities.

Code of conduct

A code of conduct is essential for the running of any event – online, offline or hybrid. Everyone should be made aware of this code of conduct from the start, and you will need moderators on hand who are clearly briefed on what action to take if someone behaves in a way that is not acceptable. This ensures a positive experience for everyone.

At WTS, we always start all events by sharing our code of conduct, The WTS Way,[4] as well as share it in advance in our countdown emails. It is also signposted in our website FAQs, and we have a QR code on holding slides that links to it so that people can refer to it throughout the event. At the beginning of online events, we share a link to The WTS Way.

It's also important that you clearly signpost, and regularly remind attendees, who they should go to if they need to report any issues.

Getting event feedback

Once the event is over, you need to have a plan for encouraging, analysing and responding to feedback. As we've seen throughout this book, feedback from your community is vital for shaping future initiatives and making sure you are meeting the needs of your audience.

There are two types of feedback you can gather. The first is quantitative data, which you can get from a simple form. You can ask event attendees to rate how satisfied they were with:

- The event overall
- Different pre-event elements, such as pricing, communication and the booking process
- Different elements of the event itself, such as venue, speakers, breaks and atmosphere
- Specific talks or sessions

You could also ask whether they would be likely to attend another event in future.

The following are a few questions we include in our WTSFest feedback form, which all require a rating between 1 to 4, where 1 is very dissatisfied and 4 is very satisfied.

- How satisfied were you with WTSFest?
- How satisfied were you with the following in the lead-up to the event?
  - Ticket price
  - Email comms
  - Event app
- How satisfied were you with the following on the event day?
  - Venue
  - Registration
  - Volunteers
  - Catering
  - Safety
  - Networking
  - Overall vibe
- If you attended the after-party, how satisfied were you with the following?
  - Venue
  - Safety
  - Variety of drinks
  - Networking
- How much did you feel our code of conduct was modelled well throughout the event?
- How likely are you to attend WTSFest again?

We then ask two free-flowing questions on what they liked best about the event and what could be done to improve the event.

We went through several iterations of our feedback forms until we settled on one that we felt works best, because of how low effort it is for the attendee to fill it, mainly relying on number rating, but also because it's easy for us as organizers to then average the scoring and compare them with previous and future events.

The other type of feedback is qualitative. This involves talking to people, either in focus groups or one-to-one interviews. At WTS, we run calls with at least one representative from each of these groups: volunteers, speakers, first-time attendees, repeat attendees and international attendees.

We ask them questions such as:

- What makes a conference experience feel like a smooth experience for you?
- What did you feel was missing from WTSFest this time round?
- What is one initiative we could add to our event day that would help people make new professional connections?
- How can we make WTSFest a more inclusive and welcoming space for all people of marginalized genders?

Once we have analysed all the feedback – both quantitative and qualitative – we send an email to all our attendees summarizing what we have learned and actions we will take in the future as a result. We then revisit this summary when planning our next event.

Deciding if events make sense for your community

Organizing and hosting events requires a lot of time, effort and attention. Some events, such as small meetups or community-led gatherings, you may want to keep exclusively for your community members, in which case you will only promote them through your community platform and channels.

However, larger events, such as conferences, you will most likely want to share publicly, as these are ways for new prospective members to discover your community. In this case, your event will need its own dedicated marketing strategy.

Central to making the promotion of your event a success is being incredibly clear on what will happen over the course of the event. You need to understand what's included in a ticket, and what's not, so that you can manage expectations. Provide as much guidance and communication as you can through emails, guides and documentation, and make sure your messaging is clear and upfront to avoid any misunderstandings.

Although I'm a huge advocate for events, I know they're not for everyone – and not every type of event will suit every type of community. You will need to experiment and find what works for you.

It's good to try different formats and learn from the experience. You might find that online webinars suit your audience best, or you might find that large-scale conferences are a huge hit with your community. You won't know until you give it a go.

The key is to get feedback throughout so that you know what went well, what didn't go well and what actions you can take off the back of it. You can also let your community guide you in the first place by asking them what they're looking for, but you also need to know that they might not realize how much they want an online book club, for example, until you create one for them, so don't be afraid to take chances.

In the next chapter, we'll tackle the challenges of managing a growing community, and the importance of ensuring that the space you're building stays a safe, positive and productive space for everyone.

Key takeaways

- Events offer your members an opportunity to build relationships with one another, strengthening their relationships with the community and with you as a brand.
- Events are a powerful way to introduce new potential members to your community and grow your membership.
- You need to decide whether you will host online, offline or hybrid events (or a combination).
- In-person events can range from small, informal meetups to large-scale conferences.

- Virtual events will likely be shorter and more focused to avoid overwhelming people with too much time and activity on a screen.
- Hybrid events combine in-person and virtual elements and require a great deal of work, but this can yield huge rewards.
- You need a clear code of conduct for your event which all attendees are regularly reminded of, and moderators need to be on hand to manage any issues.
- After your event, ensure that you encourage and take learnings from quantitative and qualitative feedback, and let your community know what actions you will take as a result.

Reflection questions

Here are some questions to help you consider your approach to events.

1 What do your members most want to get from an event? Where can you add real value?

2 What type of event would be most suited to meeting that need? Would it work best online, offline or as a hybrid event?

3 How can you involve your community in planning and executing your events?

Notes

1 Digital Community Leaders. 2023 Digital Community Leaders Survey Report, 2023, https://digitalcommunityleaders.com/ (archived at https://perma.cc/8SMN-GW2E)

2 Women in Tech SEO. WTSFest, 2024, www.womenintechseo.com/conference/ (archived at https://perma.cc/5ZJL-S8YS)

3 Evntt. Create a community for your event, 2024, www.evntt.io/ (archived at https://perma.cc/FYB8-8285)

4 Women in Tech SEO. The WTS Way, 2024, www.womenintechseo.com/code-of-conduct/ (archived at https://perma.cc/6RT7-KA5R)

Dealing with challenges   7

Bringing together a varied group of individuals is never going to be without challenges. Now that you have built a community and welcomed in engaged members, your responsibility is to ensure the space remains safe, positive and productive for everyone. Including you.

Code of conduct

In Chapter 2, we looked at the importance of creating a code of conduct that outlines the rules and values of your community, and sharing this with all members (and your team) so that they are clear on what is expected. When challenges arise, your code of conduct can guide you through. It will tell you how to moderate any issues and how to respond to behaviour that goes against your values. Without that solid foundation, when difficulties do come up, you may be left confused and on shaky ground as to what to do.

Rooting your code of conduct in your values isn't just about image or consistency. These shared values and sense of what matters are largely what brought your community together in the first place. A diverse group of members connect with one another because they feel aligned with a particular mission and approach. This is what unites them and helps them feel they have a lot in common, despite any differences.

Any new members joining the community should be asked to adhere to the code of conduct, and it needs to be stored somewhere that is accessible and easy to find, whether that is pinned in a channel, on your website or clearly linked from your community platform, so that members can refer to it at any time. But in order for your code of conduct to be effective, it can't just be something that people hear about once. It should be constantly referred back to and reinforced. Members shouldn't be left to forget about what it was they agreed to – there needs to be regular reminders that make your values and the practical application of your rules come to life.

This isn't simply a document that you will create once and then put aside. A code of conduct needs continual review and should be regularly updated. At Women in Tech SEO (WTS), our code of conduct[1] has evolved over the years, and a lot of that evolution has been shaped by challenges that have shown us the need for new rules or new values. Every issue that occurs is a learning opportunity, and a chance to develop your code of conduct. Particularly if you find yourself facing a high number of problems within a short span of time, this is an indication that you need to go back to your code of conduct and your moderation strategy (which we will talk more about in a moment) to see what changes need to be made.

Enforcement and reporting

It is critical that your code of conduct outlines exactly how the rules will be enforced. You should have a section that explicitly states what actions will be taken in the event that a member breaks a rule or does not follow the code of conduct. For example, you might choose to list the rules of the community and then state below the list that any member who breaks any of these rules will be removed from the group.

The WTS code of conduct contains the following enforcement section.

ENFORCEMENT

If a participant engages in harassing behaviour, organizers retain the right to take any actions to keep the community a welcoming environment for all participants. This includes warning the offender or expulsion from the group and or/event with no refund.

Organizers may take action to redress anything designed to, or with the clear impact of, disrupting the group and or/event or making the environment hostile for any participants. We expect participants to follow these rules at all times, including in any group-related social activities.

You should also make clear how members can report an issue that occurs within the community. It might be that they need to contact the group admin – in which case, you need to provide the details of how that person can be contacted. Managing a large community means that you are unlikely to be able to spot all problems that crop up by yourself, so it is important that your members are able to bring issues to your attention. If they don't know how to report a problem, or don't feel comfortable and confident to do so, then the environment within your community can quickly become toxic, and a number of unhappy members will head straight out the door.

The WTS code of conduct sets out the following.

REPORTING

If someone makes you or anyone else feel unsafe or unwelcome, please report it as soon as possible to our organizers. Our team will be happy to help and assist you to feel safe.

Harassment and other code of conduct violations reduce the value of our community for everyone. We want you to be happy, safe and comfortable in our group.

If you have any issues or concerns, please notify Areej AbuAli right away either via group direct messages or reach out via email: contact@womenintechseo.com

If this happens during an in-person event, please find Areej or a team member and say, 'I have an issue, can we chat?'

Reportings will remain confidential to the best of our abilities. We will work with you to make sure we handle it in a way that is most comfortable for you.

Behaviour modelling

The code of conduct is not just for members, either. It's important that the team behind the community are practising what they preach. If the people who are leading or moderating this space aren't following the code of conduct, you can't expect the members to either.

If your guidelines encourage the use of inclusive language, and you ask people, for example, to avoid gendered language, you can't then come into the space and start a post with 'Hey guys'. You need to model the inclusive language you expect from others. Similarly, if your guidelines ask members not to share promotional content, you shouldn't be heavily promotional just because it's your community.

Knut Melvær explains how behaviour modelling has brought the intention for Sanity's community to life. 'From the start, I was very determined that we wanted to build a kind place on the internet where people felt safe and welcome to ask questions. The tagline for a very long time was "there are no stupid questions". The primary way we thought about that was that we need to model that behaviour. We need to be present and show folks how you can respond.'

In WTS, we have a rule that also states 'There's no such thing as a silly or stupid question.' We encourage all questions, because we truly believe that all questions are good questions. In the early days of our community, a lot of members would begin posts with, 'Sorry, this is a stupid question' or words to that effect. So, we introduced the rule to make it clear that all questions were welcome. When further apologies were made for 'silly' questions, I would then say, 'Please remember our community rule: there's no such thing as a stupid or silly question.' Over time, my modelling of that behaviour led to other members following suit. Soon I found that, when someone apologized for asking a stupid question, before I had the chance to refer them to our community rules, another community member would already have stepped in to say, 'There's no such thing as a stupid question.'

The more you promote awareness of the rules, and the more you model the behaviour you want to see, the more your members become advocates for your code of conduct and encourage others to follow the rules.

Christina Garnett says that consistency is key – both in how you respond to behaviour, and in how you and your team behave yourselves. 'You need clearly written rules that dictate what is good and what is bad, and more importantly, you have to mirror what good behaviour looks like, and you have to amplify it because otherwise, people feel othered. The problem is the grey area where someone can say, "How is what I'm doing different than that person? Why is mine bad, but theirs is acceptable?" That, I find, is the biggest problem, and especially in today's geopolitical climate, we're seeing a lot of that.'

Aligning your behaviours with your values and your code of conduct doesn't end with your community, either. Christina points out that your behaviour outside the community will also have an impact on the group. 'For example, if it's a customer community and someone wasn't taken care of, of course, they're going to go into the community and say something along the lines of, "You double charged me and won't fix it". You have to make sure that it aligns with not just that culture you say you have, but actually what is happening.

'I'm a big proponent of the customer experience, and their journey needs to feel as warm as the community they're building. If sales are mean to them, and their customer success manager doesn't care, and then they get in the community, and the conversation is completely different, it will feel disjointed and disconnected, and it also makes people lose trust, because how can talking to sales and CSMs feel so ideologically different than the community?

'It's those little things – you have to be hyper-obsessed with the customer. You have to be hyper-obsessed with what their experience is like and whether the ideal experience happens across the entire journey. If not, where's the disconnect? Is this an issue of miscommunication? Is this something that we could fix, and what does that look like? It comes down to caring. I find that, especially for community managers, if you genuinely care about people in your community, you're going to instinctively do a lot of the right things.'

Proactive > Reactive

When it comes to moderation and community management, being proactive is a more effective strategy than being reactive.

Every now and then, in the WTS community, I will see a post or a question shared, which in itself does not break the code of conduct, and is not problematic, but is written in such a way that, proactively, I know some of the responses it may receive could end up being problematic,

Figure 7.1   Proactive vs reactive

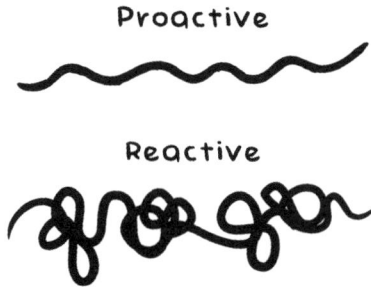

Proactive

Reactive

and may break the code of conduct. I usually take action upfront. This wouldn't be to delete the post, as the person themselves hasn't done anything wrong, but I would contact the author and have an honest conversation in which I recommend *they* remove or edit the post because similar posts in the past have resulted in negative experiences. This is something that helps to mitigate a lot of issues, and prevent a great deal of problems from arising in the first place.

Many online platforms offer settings that ensure you approve any messages before they are posted to the group. Now, of course, this takes up time and resources, but it may save you time in the long term if you don't have to regularly delete posts or manage the fall-out of problematic posts. This can be very helpful if you get a number of posts that are spammy or salesy, if this is something that is not permitted in your group. It also allows you to get in front of any issues, catching problematic posts before they are shown to your community members and any offence or discord is caused.

You can't guard against every possible issue, but the more you can be aware of what issues might crop up and why, the more you can get in front of them and limit the instances where you have to rely on reactive mechanisms.

Laura Roth emphasizes the importance of human connection in these situations. 'In general, if you speak to somebody one-on-one and just explain why something was slightly against the way that you do things, most of the time you can actually turn that negative into a positive, but you can't just ignore it. Or if it's online, deleting a comment is never a good idea without telling someone why. I think you've just got to treat your community members like you would in any human relationship. Sometimes just remind them, and then if that happens again, that's when you maybe have an issue.'

Moderation process

There are a number of ways to approach moderation. These include:

- A single community manager who takes responsibility for moderation
- A team of moderators who share responsibility
- Volunteer moderators from within the community

These moderators oversee a number of steps on the member journey, from deciding who is permitted to join and welcoming them, to overseeing the conversations taking place, deciding when to take action and potentially removing people from the group if necessary.

It's important that your moderation process is clear and transparent from the very beginning. Some communities give members a certain number of warnings – such as a 'three-strike rule', where you can be warned about behaviour that breaks the code of conduct three times before being removed from the group. Warnings can be given privately or publicly. Other communities will remove a person straight away the first time they contravene that code because it was stated from the outset that membership was predicated on adherence.

Knut Melvær says that this is the approach at Sanity: 'It's one warning. If you aren't receptive, too bad. When you join the community, we set up an automation with a welcome message and the code of conduct. If you didn't read it, it's too late.'

A model that works well in many groups is that of educating, then moderating, then removing:

1 **Educating:** raising awareness of the code of conduct and what behaviour is expected.
2 **Moderating:** letting people know where behaviour has fallen short of those expectations.

3 Removing: making the decision to dismiss someone from the group where they haven't taken on board the education and moderation feedback.

Of course, it's human nature for people, sometimes, to respond to moderation with defensiveness. That's why it's so vital to have that clear code of conduct to refer back to, and to point any members to if they're unhappy with your decision or your feedback. When you can rely on the specific rule that has been contravened, the conversation is much simpler. And it may be that in some cases, the right action to take is removal, and that goes back to your enforcement rules that are outlined in your code of conduct.

Platform moderation functionality

Many online platforms have built-in moderation features that you can use to automate some of this work. This helps ensure a consistent experience for all members and takes the pressure off the community managers.

These tools might help you by, for instance, holding posts in certain circumstances so they can be checked by a moderator before they appear publicly. If a member is brand new to the group, perhaps they joined within the last month or they haven't previously posted, then settings can be put in place so that a moderator will review and accept their post before the rest of the group is able to view it. You might wish to check every post before it is made public, but this can be onerous on your (or your team's) time. So, you may wish to enable long-standing members who regularly contribute to the community to be able to post freely without prior review.

Many platforms also allow you to ask members a series of questions before joining. Moderators can then review each individual's answers to decide whether or not they can be accepted into the group. This might be based on them promising to follow certain rules, or assessing whether they share the group's values.

One particularly helpful community feature that exists in some online groups is the ability for members to report problematic posts to an admin or a moderator so that they can review them and take the necessary action. If you're running a community of thousands of people, it is extremely difficult, if not impossible, for you to keep track of all the comments on all the posts that are happening, so being able to foster relationships with members that encourage them to flag potential issues is crucial.

Here are a few specific examples of in-platform moderation tools for Facebook Groups and Slack, the two we use in the WTS community.

Facebook groups

In Facebook groups, you can choose to make use of any of the following optional features:

- Assign admin roles to involve them in the moderation process
- Delete posts or comments
- Prevent posts from appearing from users who may be bots (for example those that have a brand-new account and/or no profile picture)
- Hold posts for moderation from users who have broken rules or had posts disapproved within the last 28 days
- Prevent posts from appearing that contain potentially problematic content, suspected spam or specific keywords
- Require *all* posts from members to be approved by a moderator before they are visible to the group
- Turn off comments on any posts where the discussion is becoming problematic, or where you suspect discussion may become problematic
- If you delete a post, share a link to the rule that the post violated
- Mute members who consistently break rules or cause conflict, as a precursor to removing them
- Admin log to note any members or posts that have been removed and reasons why so that other moderators can refer to the log when needed

Slack

In addition to its own in-built features, Slack also integrates with a number of other platforms, giving you a range of tools to use collaboratively. In Slack, you can:

- Assign admin roles to involve them in the moderation process
- Delete posts or comments
- Manage who can post in a channel
- Manage who can notify members of channels
- Set up automated responses to frequently asked questions
- Automatically message members who are using specific keywords – for example, to warn them that their content may violate rules and that they may want to rephrase their message before posting

The human touch

Moderation tools and automation are highly valuable because of the burden they take away from the admin team, and the consistency of their approach (an AI bot will respond to the same language in exactly the same way, no matter who used it). But it's important that there's a human overseeing the whole process. Technology isn't infallible, and someone needs to be checking that everything is working as it should.

As Pete Heslop, managing director of Steadfast Collective, explains, 'Clear and transparent guidelines must be the core of all moderation. Once you have your "rules", you can use tools to automatically and manually enforce them. However, as is nearly always the case, technology isn't the solution, but the tool to implement the solution.'

For Sanity, Knut Melvær explains how AI can be an asset and a potential problem – and, sometimes, just a tiny bit irritating. 'When people join our community, we make sure to try and welcome everyone. We felt it was like you're inviting people to a party. You're trying to come in the door and say, "Hey, nice to see you, and welcome in". I think that can create a feeling of, "Oh, there are humans here". The company is actually here and looks at this. The guy from the video is actually helping me out. That was important.

'Up to a point, we managed to moderate stuff manually. Then we have started using Slackbot to remind folks to use inclusive language and so on. It has been interesting because there are people from Australia to the West Coast and everything in between, right? They come with their own cultural perspectives and customs and so on. That has definitely been a learning curve. There are some cross-contextual issues we have to think about as well. We have reminders and public announcements like, "Hey, be mindful of this" and so on. We definitely have started to feel that pain with Slack and attempting to automate moderation.'

Publicly dealing with challenges

Often, it seems appropriate to talk to someone privately when an issue occurs. When a member has broken a rule, a one-to-one conversation via private message or an in-person meeting might seem more compassionate. However, this means that there are no learning opportunities for the rest of the community. Dealing with an issue publicly gives you a chance to show other members what sort of behaviour is considered problematic, and to model how problems should be dealt with.

This is not about naming and shaming – it does no good to publicly shame anyone, and you can avoid naming the individual concerned. But you can publicly post or announce that an issue has occurred, explain why it is a problem, and explain what can be done going forward so that the whole community takes responsibility for creating a positive space. It also gives you an opportunity to reiterate the code of conduct and the rules so that everyone is clear on expectations.

A public response is particularly important if a decision has been made because of the issue in question. For example, if a new rule is being added, a rule is being changed, or a new moderation process is being introduced, your members need to understand why this change is taking place and why it matters.

Let me share an example from my own experience to illustrate this point. In the WTS community, we run a mentorship programme. In one cohort in this programme, one of the mentees ghosted their mentor. Although this was an isolated instance, I shared publicly with the community that this had happened, without naming either of the people involved, so that everyone could learn from it. I also let everyone know that, going forward, we would introduce a condition in the application for the programme to state that this behaviour would result in removal from the community. This meant that everyone recognized the issues caused by this behaviour, that they understood why this new rule had been brought in and that they were more aware of the need to avoid any future such issues.

Dealing publicly with challenges can feel extremely vulnerable. But it can be done in a positive and empowering way – rather than focusing on the negative, it is about sharing learnings and enabling the community to grow together.

This approach also tends to encourage members to be more open with feedback or sharing any issues or concerns, because they feel that this is a safe space where you, as a community builder, are being open to them. They are able to trust you and are confident that you will hear and support them. Not only that, but feedback from your community on what's working and what isn't can be extremely helpful in dealing with existing challenges and mitigating future issues.

You can't make everyone happy

One thing that I have come to realize, after many years of managing communities, is that you cannot make everyone happy. Sometimes you have to make very tough decisions, like deciding that a certain person isn't a good fit for the group or is causing too many issues. Some of the rules you put in place might make most people feel they are safer and being treated fairly, but others may feel they are unreasonable or too harsh. Some people may get defensive about the feedback you provide concerning certain behaviour. It can be a difficult thing to face, and it's something that many community builders struggle with, but it is something that we all have to come to accept,

You can't make everyone happy, and that's okay.

The key is to approach issues in as unbiased a way as you can. This is a challenge, as we all have deep-seated biases, most of which are unconscious, and it takes effort to push ourselves to consider whether we are letting our own preferences or previous experiences get in the way. But the more that you can limit the impact of your personal biases, the more you can ensure you're being fair to your community. Then you are able to justify your tough decisions, because you know that you are applying your rules consistently and justly.

Sometimes being fair is more valuable than being popular. As much as you don't want to upset anyone, what you're building in your community is too important to be derailed by people-pleasing. Trying to make everyone happy usually results in no one being happy. You need to be confident in the values and rules that underpin your community so that you can focus on cultivating the culture you set out to create.

What comes next

We've now come to the end of our second section, where we covered the steps for growing your community. We started by talking about strategies for spreading the word to attract new members. We then looked at how we can retain members and keep them engaged. We also covered the importance of bringing members together through events and the different shapes they can take place in. Finally, in this chapter, we addressed how to deal with challenges that may arise as a community grows.

In the next section, we'll explore scaling your community, starting with gathering and capturing insights.

Key takeaways

- Your code of conduct will guide you through issues that arise within your community.
- New members should be required to agree to the code of conduct, and the community should be given regular reminders of the requirements.
- Your code of conduct should stipulate how rules will be enforced and how members can report any issues.
- Model the behaviour that you want to see from your members.
- A proactive approach can help to reduce the number of issues that arise.
- You need a clear, transparent and consistent moderation process.
- Make use of automated tools, but don't lose the human element.
- Dealing with challenges publicly provides learning opportunities for everyone.
- You can't please everyone, and you shouldn't try – it's more important to be fair and consistent in your decisions to safeguard the culture you are trying to build.

Reflection questions

The following questions will help you prepare for potential challenges.

1 How will issues be dealt with in your community? What will be the process for reporting problems and enforcing the code of conduct?

2 How can your team model the behaviour you want to see and remind your community of your expectations?

3 What tools and resources can you use to support you with moderation?

Note

1 Women in Tech SEO. The WTS Way, 2024, www.womenintechseo.com/code-of-conduct/ (archived at https://perma.cc/2UXQ-UP9T)

PART THREE
Scaling your community

Gathering insights 8

We've now reached a stage where you have developed a strong core community. You have laid solid foundations on which you have built an active and engaged membership. Now it's time to go big. In this section, we'll be looking at how you scale your community and make a real impact.

One way that you can take your community to the next level is through the insights that it can make available to you. Not only can these guide you in how your community should evolve to attract more members and drive more engagement, but they can also be hugely valuable to business decisions and future growth.

In this chapter, we will learn from the real-life experiences of The TEFL Org, Sanity and Buffer on how they go about gathering and capturing insights from their community.

Social listening

Social listening is the process of monitoring and analysing online conversations. It can tell you a great deal about your brand reputation, or the reputation of your competitors, and what your target audience cares about, who they are, and what they think of and need from your products. Social listening is normally conducted using a range of tools to cover multiple platforms.

However, one of the biggest draws of launching a community for many brands is that hosting your own platform means that you can listen in to a wide range of conversations directly.

There is something special about conversation that organically happens in a community without any form of prompting. This can be

Figure 8.1   Social listening

noticed when people use phrases such as 'I'm looking for...' or 'Is there...?'. These showcase what truly matters to people and what they're searching for.

With a community, you are not just tracking mentions and keywords across platforms; you are building relationships with your target audience and engaging in an ongoing dialogue with them. The people who have chosen to join your community are united by shared interests that relate directly to your brand and products, so you don't have to guess whether they might be your potential customers – you know that they are the people you need to talk to. You can learn a lot more about who they really are than any vague demographic profiling will tell you.

Sentiment analysis – understanding whether people have a broadly positive or negative view of your brand or products – is notoriously challenging using standard tools, as it relies on monitoring of keywords that can vary depending on context. And bots don't understand sarcasm. But when you are immersed in real conversations and building real relationships, you can get a much more accurate understanding of people's genuine views and feelings. You will also find, as we've seen in previous chapters, that they will begin to open up to you and provide feedback that they might not have shared anywhere else.

The value of listening

This connection to your audience can be a huge advantage over your competitors. If they are coming to you with feedback, needs or requests that other brands aren't hearing about, you can be the first, and most effective, to solve their problems. You can also solicit insights that enable you to improve your existing products in order to make your current customers happier, so you retain more of them, and attract more new customers.

In the Women in Tech SEO (WTS) community, we work closely with our partners to understand some of the common challenges and questions that are being shared by our community members. If we find that many of our members have a common challenge in finding a tool that helps make a part of their job more efficient, then we communicate that with our SaaS partners as a potential feature that can be built by one of them. Another way is to collate some of the common questions shared and work on building out a content guide or resource that helps answer these questions. For example, we noticed that one of the topics that get the most questions is on JavaScript SEO, and we decided to run a free training course for our community members on this exact topic; it received the largest number of sign-ups we've had for any webinar we've run before.

Another opportunity is to use this group as beta testers. Your community becomes your VIP users, who can test new products or developments to provide feedback that enables you to perfect your offering before you release it more widely.

At The TEFL Org, Alan Moir says their community insights were invaluable in understanding how to progress graduates onto their Business English course. 'We gave them access to the first unit and we were saying, "What do you think of the layout, the way it's spaced out in terms of video, text content, the assessment? Is this what you'd expect or would you expect something else? In terms of feedback, is this what you were expecting? If we call it this, if it includes this, what is missing? What do we need to add?", that sort of thing. Then, that went into informing the design, whether we need to make the modules or the unit shorter or include more video content or content that isn't so text heavy. With an online course, you don't want someone just sitting in front of a screen clicking. You want it to be as engaging as possible.'

Customer insight vs market research

An important point to note is the difference between customer insight and market research. Customer insight focuses on understanding the needs of your customers, whereas market research takes a wider view of the whole market. This can give you a broad understanding, but it is likely to be vaguer and more generic than anything that comes from your actual clientele. The more information you can get on what the people who actually buy from you are looking for, the better.

Not only do customer insights give you useful guidance, but they also help your customers feel valued. When people see that their feedback drives real change and development, they will be far more loyal and connected to your brand.

Customer insights are not always simply about your product. When you are a part of the conversations your customers are having, you will learn about particular challenges they are having in their day-to-day lives that might spark ideas for ways that you can support them. You might see people asking their fellow members for recommendations of tools or platforms that fulfil a particular need, which will inspire developments for your future growth.

Customer insights also help give you a better idea of brand awareness and can even be used to measure it. At WTS, we run a quarterly survey where we list out all our community partner names and ask our members to rate how well they know them, scoring between 1 to 4, where 1 they know nothing about them and 4 they know a lot about them. Running this every quarter helps form a picture of how a partner's brand awareness changes over time and helps us measure how successful our quarterly initiatives are with our partners. It's worth noting that this requires having an engaged community, for them to agree to take part in a quarterly survey. If your members know that there's benefit coming off the back of the work you do with partners, then they'll organically take part. We talk more about the value of partnering up with communities in the next chapter.

Influencing your roadmap

We previously discussed the need to prioritize initiatives based on impact and effort, but another key element in planning your roadmap is understanding what your customers are looking for.

At Buffer, users directly influence their roadmap for product development through their Buffer Suggestions tool.[1] Their roadmap is entirely transparent and visible to all, and users can vote and comment on new feature ideas, as well as submit their own. Buffer says, 'Our community is eager to help us improve, and it's an absolute blessing.'[2] This is an approach that we can all take to heart. At the end of the day, building what your customers really want will always be a more successful approach than building what you think is a good idea or what seems cost-effective.

For Sanity, Knut Melvær says, 'We are a bit precious about our roadmaps because we are worried about committing to something that we steer away from. It's always founded on customer and community feedback, for sure, but not determined by it. We try to work on the right thing.'

Accessing insights directly from your customers removes the need for costly and time-consuming product iterations and usability testing. The initial conversations with your customers can direct you to build a highly tailored and effective first version that responds directly to their needs.

Capturing community insights

So, how do you capture and document these insights? How do you ensure that they're acted on? There are many different approaches you can take, so here I would like to share two examples of how real businesses do it.

Sanity

Sanity knows that customer insights are vital. Knut Melvær admits that, in Sanity's early days, the community were often quicker to spot issues and bugs than the team themselves, and credits them with helping the business move on to the next level, as well as being crucial to their future growth. 'As we have gone from being a startup to what you can call a scale-up, a lot of our maturing has been to better capture customer feedback. I feel that now we have a job to do in having better processes, formal processes, around capturing all the community feedback. Because there's a lot of things that are reported that I can look at and have a feeling of what's going on, but it's not very tangible in a way.'

The next stage of the journey, for Knut and his team, is figuring out how to use those insights more effectively, and they are considering several possibilities. 'I feel like every week there are software tools that try to sell me this solution, but we can probably leverage AI to look at the corpus of messages that float through our Slack. It would be interesting to see if that's feasible. Or looking at GitHub issues and sorting them after how many reactions or comments they have. Or even simple searches in the community, to find patterns. We haven't figured that out yet.'

The area where customer insights are most effective for Sanity right now is in product testing. 'When things are getting ready, or in alpha or beta, we invite people from the community to try it out and give us feedback. We also recruit people from the community for UX research.'

Buffer

Joel Gascoigne says that Buffer Suggestions, which we introduced earlier, has gone through a few iterations to ensure that the process is as effective as possible, 'We had quite a few years where we had a survey that someone could fill out and we would receive that. We did read every one of them and we tried our best to incorporate it into the roadmap. Interestingly, we ended up doing a lot of work just to manage all the requests coming in. They would go into a spreadsheet but then we'd have to analyse what type of a request it was, maybe put it into different categories, and essentially come up with several priority levels for each thing.

'The great thing with Buffer Suggestions is that it's public and people can go and browse and then they can vote on anything that they would like to see us build. Then some comments are public as well. This helps hold us accountable. If something's at the top of the list, there's no way we can ignore it because we've got that public accountability element. If we didn't manage this channel or respond to people or if we left something at the top and didn't work on it for two years, that would look very bad. It incentivizes us to respond and move it along and probably, in most cases, start working on it.'

As the process has improved, it has also become less time-consuming and complex for the team, making it easier to manage and implement. Joel says, 'Essentially there's some moderation that we do in the background and sometimes there's duplicate requests that are submitted by people where they didn't see one, but it's easy to merge requests and then the votes just get increased. We have one of our staff product managers managing all of that, but it's really eliminating a lot of organizational work that we were doing before, and then we didn't get all these other benefits of the community, the sense of trust and transparency, reliability that comes from just browsing. I think just the act of browsing and saying, "Oh, what are other people interested in?" is something powerful with an emotional impact for people.'

The success of Buffer Suggestions has inspired the team to seek customer insights at later stages of the development process, too. 'I've been thinking about it as embedding customers in our workflows in a very tangible way. That's why we introduced an open beta program. Within someone's Buffer account settings, they can opt into the beta program. Every new feature that we're building, we put it into beta for some time. When you opt into the beta program, you're going to get access to things early. The only catch is we want your feedback – we want to hear from you. We're working towards having customers testing things out for several weeks before we roll them out to everyone and then really being committed to making changes based on what they're sharing with us. It's interesting because it gets customers embedded in our processes. It arguably improves what we end up building. It's going to be better quality for those insights.'

Joel says this customer involvement makes the community much more excited and enthusiastic about the products, helping them to launch more successfully. 'If we put things in beta early enough, which we're pushing earlier and earlier and earlier, then it's almost inevitable that we will make some changes because we're doing it early enough that it's not completely polished yet. Then we end up with community members that have shared things with us and then we've made changes based on that which have made tangible differences to what we end up building. Those people, of course, feel invested in us and connected with us. When it comes to the time to launch that feature to everyone, they're going to be cheering us on and probably sharing it with their networks at the same time because they feel that, "Oh, yes, I'm part of this and I get to shape things".'

Ensuring that the team are connected to this work is vital to making sure these customer insights are utilized. Joel explains, 'There are so many ways that we're getting the community embedded in our workflows. From a customer perspective, it's typical for them to feel their requests go into a black hole and they don't know how it's going to be used if it's going to be used, and they don't know what others are suggesting. This is why Buffer Suggestions is great, it's primarily owned by the Product team, and it makes our customers feel this sense of trust because of how transparent the process is. It helps get the Product team embedded with customers. We need to treat it as a shared responsibility. That's how I think about it and put the work in to make that work.'

Enabling that relationship between different teams and your customers means that customer research can become an ongoing, fluid process that happens throughout product development, rather than focus groups or surveys at specific points, as Buffer's example shows.

'One of the reasons I feel strongly about it being a shared responsibility,' says Joel, 'is that on the product side, if you can jump into a warm conversation with someone who's already got in touch with us, either through customer support, through email, or just in our Discord community, and they're talking specifically about one part of the product that happens to be part of something the team is working on, then it's the perfect coincidence.

'This customer is already interested. We have an active conversation and if they can just jump in on that, they could probably also ask, "Hey, would you mind jumping on a half an hour Zoom and talking about it more and sharing your screen and walking me through what you'd love to see here?" Suddenly we can just jump into customer research mode essentially, which is what they want to be doing regularly.'

Creating opportunities for customers to provide actionable insights is fantastic, but you also need to make sure your customers *know* that they can provide insights and how to do so. Joel says that this has been steadily improving at Buffer, and one-to-one conversations with the customer service team have been key to building momentum.

'They've been receiving feature requests from people for years and years. With Buffer Suggestions, it's great because they can send someone a link to the page for that feature request. When someone mentions something, we can send that over and say, "Hey, do you want to add your vote here? Then it'll get built faster, essentially". That's definitely a way.'

But Buffer is also utilizing a range of other channels, and, crucially, within the Buffer platform itself. 'Through email, customer service, also through social media. That's where we are making people aware of it. We also actually have it in the product, so right within Buffer – it's just in one of our drop-down menus inside the product. You can go to 'help' and then suggest a feature and it'll take you right there.'

Those community insights aren't just valuable for informing your next steps, either. Joel gives an example that shows how they can also guide partner organizations to help you build something that your customers want, supporting your retention and acquisition. 'For example, in 2024, adding Meta Threads to Buffer was our top request. Inside the Buffer platform, there's an area in your settings where you can go and connect new channels. Because Meta Threads had been so popular and being requested, we decided to add it there because that's where a lot of people are going and seeing what channels we support. Since we knew that it was in a lot of people's minds, we decided to put a little section within the product where it'll show you that Threads is on the list. It says, "Coming soon." Then we have a button that says "Notify me" that's connected with Buffer Suggestions.

'We then learned that the Meta Threads team themselves, who are working on the API which would allow us to connect it, had discovered the Buffer Suggestions page and they were surprised how many people were interested in it. This helps us to then be top of their list of the products that they'll give access to the API when they come out with it. There's a lot of these virtuous circles where involving the community and doing it in a way where they're genuinely embedded shows that we value their input, and then good things come from it.'

Incentivizing insights

Often, brands will offer customers some kind of incentive in exchange for their feedback or insights. A voucher for a global retailer, an entry into a prize draw, a free month of product access or something similar. This can very often feel like the only way to encourage customers to part with their input (and the time it takes them to provide it), but it's not necessarily the best way. How meaningful is their input likely to be if they're only doing it for a shopping voucher?

At Buffer, Joel is not keen on incentives at all, but, luckily, their engaged community means that they don't need to offer any gimmicks. 'I feel very strongly that we don't do it, but, interestingly, there's been points of time where maybe a new product designer has joined, and they want to get that feedback from customers, but they felt that barrier because we didn't have the community in place and we didn't have those habits in place, yet they still needed the feedback. So, they end up going out on their own and doing all that work themselves to find people, and they're like, "Well, I need to offer them something because I'm emailing them cold". I think that's where you end up doing those things. Whereas if you have a strong community and you have a strong brand, and you're committed to investing in that community and you care about their involvement in the process, then I believe that you don't need to offer them anything because they're already getting something, and they organically want to be involved in that way.

'The best thing for them is that they feel like they can impact the direction and shape things, and they can ask for things that are important to them knowing we will likely consider them.'

This is a key measure of success for your community – when you can ask questions and easily get in-depth input that your audience is eager to give, without expecting anything in return. Joel agrees and highlights the fact that sometimes having a smaller community can be more of an asset than a large one if it is more engaged and provides higher quality insights.

'It's something that I've reflected on because I have gone through the experience of having this strong and vibrant community, losing a little bit in that dip of having a weaker community is where I think we started to see those things pop up more. We have sent out some of those emails, and I cringed because I knew back from when we had a small community, not only that we didn't need to do it, but the quality of input we got was higher with not doing it. Now, we're paying and offering something and getting low quality input anyway.'

Whereas Sanity do offer incentives sometimes, Knut Melvær says that the most valuable feedback often comes from 'the fans for whom it's incentive enough to get to try the new thing'. Sanity are developing an Ambassador programme to celebrate those fans.

'It's something we have talked a lot about: how can we elevate these ambassadors and people who want to tell stories about Sanity? We have talked about doing it through coaching, and giving feedback on talk proposals, videos and guides. As well as the usual, send exclusive swag, early access, and similar. We also have a community plan that gives you more bandwidth and API requests. You try to find things like that and give it to people who are doing cool things.'

It won't always be the same

Different approaches work for different brands, and often it is a process of trial and error to find what resonates with your community. The more insights you gather about your customers that help you understand them better, the more effectively you will be able to build a relationship that encourages them to share valuable insights that benefit your products.

In the next chapter, we'll explore how forming partnerships with relevant organizations can enhance your community building efforts and strengthen your brand.

Key takeaways

- Social listening is the process of monitoring and analysing online conversations, and is incredibly valuable for understanding the needs and concerns of your target audience.

- Building a community enables you to participate in and observe in-depth conversations that give you much more useful and detailed insights than standard social listening tools.

- Your community can help you understand how to improve products or services, and what products to develop next.

- Community members can act as beta testers for new products, providing useful feedback throughout the development process.

- Customers need to see that their feedback has led to tangible outcomes, or they will become disengaged.

- Seeing their feedback leading to developments and new products increases brand loyalty and advocacy.

- You need a system for capturing insights and monitoring what actions have been taken.

- You can choose to incentivize customer insights, but often the feedback is more valuable when your community are intrinsically motivated to provide it – celebrating and supporting those who do offer feedback helps encourage that behaviour.

Reflection questions

Let's look at how you can put your learnings from this chapter into practice:

1 How will you listen to your customers and community members?

2 Can you involve your community members in testing or trialling new products or developments?

3 How will you document and keep track of the insights shared in your community?

Notes

1 Buffer. All posts, nd, https://suggestions.buffer.com/ (archived at https://perma.cc/LW9H-JC9S)

2 M Eckstein. Introducing Our New Roadmap: Buffer Suggestions, 9 August 2023, https://buffer.com/resources/transparent-product-roadmap-v2/ (archived at https://perma.cc/ZA2G-E33A)

Developing partnerships

9

In this chapter, we'll look at the ways that working with relevant organizations can help build and strengthen your community – and therefore your brand.

As you work on developing your community, it may be a relief to know that you don't need to do it all alone. You don't necessarily need to start from scratch – partnerships offer you a way to tap into existing communities that align with your values and goals.

The best way to understand how partnerships can work effectively is by looking at them in action, so, in this chapter, we'll focus on a case study with software company, Moz. At Women in Tech SEO (WTS), we have a strong partnership with Moz, and I have long been impressed with the collaborative partnerships they have with other organizations. As Joelle Irvine, strategic marketing executive and former director of brand marketing at Moz, explains, 'In its early days, Moz was very much built on community and education. They've carried that through the years. It's something that they pay close attention to and something they feel is important in the industry. It's important for them to be part of that. It's something that everyone, throughout the company, is invested in.'

Don't reinvent the wheel

Many brands start off thinking that they need to build a community from the ground up by themselves, finding their target audience and driving engagement out of nothing. They soon discover that this is a huge amount of work, and that it requires a great deal of time, budget and resources, as well as a dedicated team to manage it. It can feel like a completely overwhelming task.

However, you don't need to start completely from square one. Communities already exist that attract and engage your target audience. They might be run by other businesses, they might be independent communities, professional communities or local communities. Partnering with them enables you to connect with that audience, and take advantage of their existing setup. This can be a great way to get started, as well as a way to reach and build credibility with your target audience.

There are a number of different ways to collaborate with other communities, including:

- **Formal partnership programmes:** at WTS, we offer structured arrangements that businesses can sign up to that we call WTSPartner.[1] These have defined terms, outlining what businesses will get in return for supporting us, and a fixed pricing structure.

- **Sponsorship:** you can sponsor an event or initiative organized by another community. This way the burden of organization and promotion is taken up by someone else, and therefore doesn't sit on your shoulders, but you are able to be present within the event or initiative, connecting with the audience, increasing brand awareness and driving lead generation. This is also a great way to test certain events, locations or initiatives to see whether these are the right ways and places to connect with your target audience before investing time and energy in creating something yourself.

- **Campaign collaboration:** working together on a campaign can involve creating content together, and involving the community in contributing to content that can be shared more widely, such as on your website and social media channels, as well as on those of your partner.

Partnerships can teach you valuable lessons that you can take back to your own community. Working with a partner gives you opportunities to try different initiatives, types of content, ways of engaging your community and all sorts of elements, which, if successful, you might be able to implement in your own way with your own members.

You might even find that, if a community is a perfect fit and already has everything you need, you might want to acquire it for your brand. Trialling a partnership first can enable you to check that an acquisition is the right way to go, and allow the existing membership to get used to your brand before any major transition begins.

The best partnerships are usually with brands that offer services that are closely aligned with yours and that respond to an adjacent need, but which you don't specifically offer. Or that offer the same services as you but in different locations. This not only allows you to come together in a way that provides a seamless and connected offering for your audience, but it also makes acquisitions very attractive.

Don't feel that, just because a community might be run by a 'competitor', that you can't partner with them. Often, customers are not choosing between you and other brands, they are using services from both of you. By recognizing this, both brands can open themselves up to a wider audience and demonstrate values of collaboration over competition, which are likely to be more attractive to your target customers.

Who to partner with

The first consideration in choosing a potential partner is whether they are aligned with your values. Any community that you connect with should have a similar culture and approach so that you are able to work in alignment.

The Digital Community Leaders Survey Report explains that 'You can't be everywhere, so be present where it matters most. Select the online communities, themes and territories that align with your business goals.'

Joelle Irvine explains how Moz and WTS came to work together. 'Even before I started at Moz, I was a huge admirer and supporter of the WTS community. On the Moz Marketing team, many of us were already part of the community, and we're all big supporters of the community. It was just a natural fit for us right from the get-go. Most importantly, we really love partnering with WTS because our cultures align.

'We like to find partners who are aligned with our mission and our vision. That just makes it much easier. Part of the goals that we have when we partner with folks is that, obviously, there are some advantages to increasing your audience size, but that's not really our main goal. It's more about providing people with more opportunities to contribute to our content, to be part of the discussions and be part of the voices in our channels.'

This is a reminder of the importance of setting a clear vision and values, as we looked at in Chapter 2. If you understand what you stand for as a community, it will be much easier to choose partners that are a good fit, and that will help you to achieve your goals. A well-aligned partnership also reinforces your values to your community, showing that you mean what you say and clarifying what is expected of them.

Joelle agrees, and the approach they take at Moz shows how important it is to make your values clear and transparent if you want to attract big partnerships. 'If you understand what that community is about and what their goals are, then, if your goals are aligned, it's a really easy conversation to have. Then you can move forward together. If it's not 100 per cent clear and you can't see it right off the bat, then there are questions that arise. "Does this make sense for us? Should we be doing this right now? Do we need to research a little bit more?"'

As Joelle mentioned, many of the Moz team were already members of the WTS community before deciding to partner with us. Partnering with a community that you already know well, or joining and getting to know a community you are considering partnering with, means you can see what's happening there and experience the culture for yourself in order to know for sure whether it's a good fit. And, when you're already connected with a community, both parties are more invested in making the partnership a success. Joelle comments, 'We want to make sure that we can support the people around us to be successful. We have the infrastructure and the platform for it. I think it's a nice tie-in so that it's like we're helping each other. That's what community is all about. It's about really working together, about helping each other, about becoming in sync.'

How partnerships can help

The main motivation for partnering with an existing community is to reach an audience that you aren't currently reaching. By connecting with another organization's members, you can get in front of this audience and begin a relationship with them.

The Digital Community Leaders Survey Report[2] highlights that once you have determined which communities you will partner up with, 'you can begin to craft exactly how content and community engagement will help you achieve your strategy. Establishing clear goals will ensure you are able to evaluate your impact.'

At WTS, our partners are:

- Featured on our WTSPartner landing page, displaying their name and logo with their website link
- Mentioned monthly via our social media channels, sharing any information they want to promote (such as a blog post, job advert, service promotion, etc.)
- Mentioned monthly on our private community groups, again, sharing any information they wish to promote

But, beyond that, becoming a partner with our community means that they become an extension of our team. The partnership supports brands with:

- **Marketing:** engaging and building relationships with a specific and hyper-focused group of people who share common interests, values and goals within our niche. We offer 'always-on' digital opportunities, as well as regular in-person opportunities throughout the year.
- **Sales:** we share exclusive offers and discounts for our members' products and services with a highly relevant audience.
- **Product:** our partners can tap into our community for user research, gathering feedback and understanding the needs of their target market.

- **Recruitment:** our partners have hired lots of candidates by sharing their job vacancies directly with our community members.

- **Training:** partners have access to our mentorship programme, workshops, conferences and more. Partners often report that their teams return from our events feeling motivated and inspired.

Our partnerships are built on a symbiotic relationship between our community members and partner brands. We work with partners to find the intersection of how our community members find value in their brand and how the brand can find value in our community members.

We provide connection, opportunities, education and amplification touchpoints for our partners and WTS community members. Our partners can collaborate with WTS, WTS community members or even other WTSPartners on research, content, webinars, workshops, trainings, events, podcasts and more. We also enable our partners to share knowledge and thought leadership with our community.

Not only that, but promoting that they are a WTSPartner makes a clear statement about the brand's values and demonstrates a commitment to supporting underrepresented people in our industry. This strengthens their reputation and shows that they are willing to, quite literally, put their money where their mouth is when it comes to their values.

Partnerships can amplify your content to a wider audience and encourage more people to engage with it. They can send more traffic and more pairs of eyes to your channels, platforms and tools. Your partner organization has built up a great deal of trust with their community, so when they recommend or promote you to that audience, it is a highly impactful endorsement. Partnerships can also support you with social listening, enabling you to access a whole new group of people to gather the kind of insights, support and feedback that we discussed in Chapter 8.

At Moz, Joelle says this kind of insight gathering is a key part of the work they do with their own community and with partners. 'It's important that we adapt our messaging to different channels, of course, because different people are at different places in their lives, and what they want out of things. What we try to do as much as possible is, when we communicate with our customers, which are one community essentially, what are their challenges? What do they need? What do they like? We adapt our messaging there.

'We also use that information to help with our product features. We relay that information back to the Product Team and we try to make improvements. In terms of communication outwards into the world, it's about looking at, yes, the content that we produce, but also what are the questions that people are asking? If people are asking certain types of questions and we don't have the content to support that, we look at it and say, "How can we address this?" It's not always new content. Maybe it's a small update in our content pieces. It's, how can we improve our current content?'

Connecting with a community is very different from using standard marketing channels to try to connect with an audience. For Joelle, this is a shift from broadcasting content to interacting with people. 'Back in the day, I would say it was almost like a publishing cadence. "I have to publish this. I need to distribute this case study. I need to share this with the world." Now it's more about the conversations and the insights that you get from those conversations, the outcomes that you get from those conversations, the next steps that come from those conversations, because those conversations lead to ideas on both sides, where you can then take those into new things that you're doing.'

This also involves a shift in mindset from seeing what you're doing as marketing specifically for your business to building relationships that can be mutually beneficial. Joelle says, 'I don't believe community exists in a vacuum either. It's not just online – it's online, it's in-person, it's in those one-on-one conversations that you have with folks on the side. It's the "I'm struggling with this, can you help me?" type of situation, or "I'm starting a new business, can I get some advice? Do you know anyone?" It's about connecting people. It's about having those conversations. That's the definition of community. It's very much how everything is integrated and connected in a web.'

But just because other parties are deriving benefit from the activity, too, that doesn't dilute the positive impact for your business. In fact, it enhances it, because a partnership doesn't simply promote your brand or product, it gets people actively involved with it. Joelle cites the example of Moz's Whiteboard Fridays. These are a series of educational videos that answer a specific question relevant to Moz's audience of search engine optimization professionals and content marketers. In the pre-pandemic era, these videos were filmed at Moz's office in Seattle, but the Covid-19 lockdowns forced them to reevaluate. The team began to create them remotely, and they generated connections among a community that suddenly all found themselves very isolated. When the world opened back up again, Moz's head of content, Jo Cameron, decided to take Whiteboard Fridays on the road, using partnerships to bring the creation of the videos to a range of different events (including one with WTS). Joelle comments, 'Jo essentially built it on communities around us. She would go and talk to the event organizers and say, "This is something I want to do," and they collaborated on it. That's where the magic happens. You have this idea of, "This is what I want to do. I think this is a great way to achieve that. We can actually leverage that community experience, and take it one level higher." People love Whiteboard Fridays, and they want to participate. That's how we're able to amplify new voices and new perspectives, not limited to only people who can show up in Seattle.'

For Joelle, there is a clear impact from the community on how initiatives like Whiteboard Fridays have developed, but also on how the whole business is moving forward: 'Things that we do, there's always an evolution. I feel like the evolutions that are happening right now are due to the impact of community.'

It's a two-way relationship

As we've seen, community marketing isn't about broadcasting your content. Instead of simply putting messages out into the world, you are taking part in a conversation. And this is no less true of working in partnership. Too often, marketers expect that simply putting some money into an external community is enough to ensure that they will take on the work for them. To make the partnership a success, you still need to put time and resources into working *with* your partner.

Figure 9.1 Two-way relationship

Their community then becomes an extension of the work you are doing, and you are an active participant in what is happening.

Communities are built on trust, and community builders have worked hard to make sure their members can trust them. So, they expect their partners to collaborate with them and their members to maintain their trust by adhering to their values and code of conduct.

When I asked Joelle which partnerships had been the most effective that she had worked on, she was quick to answer that it was the ones where there was a two-way relationship and active collaboration: 'I've been in places where it's, like, "Hey, can you just amplify this?" There isn't any conversation. Having things where we're working together, where we can have those conversations and see how we can do things better or work together, that's where the magic happens.'

Getting to that position takes work, and Joelle emphasizes that businesses need to be prepared to invest in their communities: 'Communities do not happen overnight, as we well know. They take effort, they take resources, they take thoughts. Adapting to that reality and making sure that you're thoughtful about the way you approach it is so important.'

For Joelle, the reason Moz have been able to build up a strong community is because the team is so fully embedded in that community and in partner communities, building those relationships: 'I feel like the team is really everywhere. Yes, they produce amazing content, but they're really embedded in the community. They're speaking to folks.'

The investment required to make communities and partnerships successful isn't merely a financial one; it's time, effort and genuine care.

Pete Heslop has listed four main reasons that community marketing initiatives fail,[3] and I think they are particularly relevant to partnerships:

1 **Impatience for results:** give it time for the relationship to grow and blossom, don't expect results overnight.

2 **Treating members like consumers:** if you simply bombard a community's members with marketing messages, they will switch off.

3 **Lack of operational support:** you need to put effort and resource into any community you set up, and the same is true of any partnership you embark on.

4 **Failing to measure and adapt:** you need to understand what success looks like, and how you will measure it.

Defining success

We talked already about aligning your goals for your own community to your 'why' behind it all, and to your values – how you measure the success of a partnership is no different.

It's important to set expectations upfront for both parties as to what success looks like, setting the key metrics that you want to achieve. Having specific KPIs for the partnership helps you both track your progress as you go along and identify any changes that need to be made. Setting points throughout the project to review these measures and discuss any learnings will be highly beneficial, rather than waiting until the end to see whether or not the partnership was a success, by which time it is too late to change anything.

For Joelle, success is strongly linked to engagement, and a partnership that doesn't offer that is one that would be considered unsuccessful: 'When a community is not hyper-engaged with us, if the excitement and engagement is more one-sided from us, generally speaking, we find it's not generally a good fit because we want to make sure whoever we partner with is as engaged and interested in a good partnership as we are.'

The actual metrics they use to measure success vary from project to project, but there is a mixture of hard numbers and more intangible elements. 'In terms of the subjective side of things,' says Joelle, 'it's the vision, it's the goals, the things to make sure we're all aligned, to make sure that there's engagement on both sides. In terms of the measured success, things like equity in speaker selection for MozCon – that is also how we measure ourselves to make sure that we hold ourselves accountable. That the content that we produce is not just the same faces all the time. We also measure success with actual numbers, such as views and visits. We also look at assisted conversions and so on from our content. It's multi-layered, I would say.'

One major reason for an organization to enter into a partnership is to increase brand awareness, but this can be a hard factor to measure. Joelle says Moz looks at who is talking about them: 'I think you can clearly see it in mentions. For example, if you look at any type of social engagement where people are mentioning the Moz brand, that's an indicator; within communities, newsletters, sharing Moz content.'

Measuring success also helps you secure budget for similar projects in future. Moz are keen to invest in partnerships because they know they work. As Joelle says, 'For Moz, it falls within the brand budget. It makes space for it because we see the value in it. It helps us achieve our goals in terms of content and distribution, but also in terms of making sure that we have a good balance of representation within our content. Because we're part of the community, we can have conversations within the community. There are moments where we amplify, for example, our blog pitch form or a call to pitch for our podcast or webinars. Having the exposure within the community allows more people to see it, and because there's already a trust factor within the community, people are more inclined to say, "Yes, I'm interested in participating in this because I could trust this community. Therefore, I can also build trust with Moz."'

It's okay if it doesn't work out

At the end of the day, however, even when you've put time, effort and money into a partnership and you've approached everything in the best way possible, sometimes it simply won't work out.

Partnerships involve a certain level of experimentation, and you will need to try different approaches, different communities and different mechanisms to find the ones that work for you.

Over the years, I've been involved in several conversations with brands who felt it doesn't make sense for them to invest in being a partner to an external community because they don't have the time or resources to give it the attention it needs, or because they want to invest in other forms of marketing.

You may also realize that your efforts should be spent on developing your own community, as opposed to partnering with other communities. The good news is, through your work partnering up with other communities, you will be better prepared to grow your own community having seen what works and what doesn't work.

Every experience you have provides you with learnings that you can take forward to the next project, so don't be disheartened when a partnership doesn't deliver everything you'd hoped for. When you find the right fit, the benefits will be well worth it.

In the next chapter, we'll be looking more at how you can use your experiences to adapt, as we get to grips with navigating change.

Key takeaways

- Other people have already built communities among the key audiences you are trying to reach – collaborating with them gives you a head start rather than trying to build your own from scratch.

- Any partner you work with should be aligned with your values and mission.

- Partnerships can help you reach audiences that you aren't currently connecting with – for reach and engagement, and for insights, feedback and social listening.

- Partnerships can support your marketing efforts, but can also help with broader business areas such as recruitment, training and product development.

- A partnership should be a two-way relationship, where your organization and your partner actively collaborate with one another.

- Partnerships can help you to diversify your initiatives and reach more diverse audiences.
- You need to set expectations from the beginning as to what success looks like and what you will measure.
- It's okay if a partnership doesn't work out – this is a process of experimentation and learning.

Reflection questions

Here are some questions to guide your thinking about partnerships:

1 What communities are already serving your target audience(s)?

2 What benefits would you be looking for from a partnership? What could you offer to the community?

3 What would success look like from a partnership?

Notes

1 Women in Tech SEO. Community Partners, 2024, www.womenintechseo.com/partners/ (archived at https://perma. cc/3BM8-BSWK)

2 Digital Community Leaders. 2023 Digital Community Leaders Survey Report, 2023, https://digitalcommunityleaders.com/ (archived at https:// perma.cc/JC63-TR7C)

3 Pete Heslop. LinkedIn, 13 August 2024, www.linkedin.com/posts/ pwheslop_why-does-community-led-marketing-fail-i-activity-7229019090776961024-BTOR/ (archived at https://perma.cc/AGH5-432Q)

Navigating change   10

When you reach the stage of scaling your community, you may feel that you've hit a groove. Engagement is strong, new members are steadily arriving, events are taking place and everything seems to be flowing. You feel ready to scale and move on to the next level. Unfortunately, this is usually the point where change arrives.

Scaling up a community often brings new challenges, from hitting a membership ceiling beyond which you struggle to grow the community, to managing an increasingly diverse group of people with varied needs and expectations, to finding that larger numbers of people can actually result in a reduction in engagement. A scaling community also needs to change, as it needs to adapt to new requirements – accommodating larger groups, possibly in more countries; introducing new initiatives and greater variety; growing the team to handle the bigger community; increased support and functionality needs; and so much more.

Change can be scary, and it can be hard to let go of how things were before. So, in this chapter, we'll look at how you can navigate change confidently and positively. We'll explore the different types of change that you might face, and strategies to help you respond.

Types of changes

Richard Millington, in 'How to develop a community strategy',[1] identifies three main types of change that community builders are likely to face:

- Community goals
- Stakeholders
- Resources

I would also like to add a fourth category of external factors. We will look at the types of changes in each of these categories below.

External factors

Changes in your industry

In our fast-paced, ever-changing world, industries are continually evolving, and sometimes a shift in focus might mean that a particular niche you have carved out begins to be less relevant, or the specific audience you have been serving begins to change or fade away.

Starting with a defined niche is a great idea to help you stand out and be clear on who you're appealing to and why. But, over time, you may want to expand. Women in Tech SEO (WTS), as the name suggests, was originally all about technical SEO. However, as we have grown, we have begun to integrate different disciplines of digital marketing. We've introduced new channels, diversified the content of our conference topics and created groups around different areas.

It's also possible that you might have the opposite experience – you realize that your community is too general, and you want to make it more specific in order to provide a stronger reason for a defined audience to join and engage with you. You can start by creating more specific channels, and holding events around specific topics to cater to niche interests and draw people in.

One change that looks set to affect almost every industry in the coming years is AI. As more businesses and functions make use of evolving technology, the roles of your audience and the way they work are likely to shift, which might mean you need to adapt the focus of the content and topics you offer them. Your community can help guide you in what changes they need if you maintain a dialogue with them and encourage regular input.

Global changes

Since 2020, we're probably more aware than ever that global events can have a significant impact on the way we all do business. But the impact isn't always a negative one.

Community grew substantially in the wake of the Covid-19 pandemic, as people found themselves eager for connection once they were thrust into lockdown. Online communities, of course, experienced the biggest growth because, for a considerable amount of 2020–2021, the only option for connection was online. While in-person communities were in high demand after the lockdown periods ended, they struggled for a long time while meeting in-person wasn't possible. The ones that survived were those that were able to diversify and find ways to support and bring together their members virtually – for some, this also meant growing their communities by reaching and enabling access for wider audiences.

Virtual communities that sprung up during the pandemic then experienced the opposite problem when the world opened back up and people were keen for offline interaction once again. Certain technology providers, like video conferencing platforms, that experienced a huge boom during lockdown, saw a dip in usage. Expressions like having 'Zoom fatigue' or being 'Zoomed out' have entered our vocabulary, as people felt exhausted from time spent in virtual meetings.

A lot of platforms and communities found during the pandemic that online events and webinars enabled them to reach much wider audiences, and participation soared as people were able to easily dial into virtual groups and talks from home. However, once people started going back into the office and spending time outside the home again, they weren't able to join all these virtual events, and participation declined again.

Again, these organizations had to adapt and think about how they could serve their audience in a broader way. Where we are aware that our community is reliant on a particular type of behaviour or situation, we need to have a plan for how we will adapt if things change and we can no longer operate as normal.

Another factor that has been very much in the public consciousness over the last few years is global conflicts and domestic unrest. When wars or protests break out, how will you handle that as a community leader? Checking in on your members and asking how everyone is doing is a great first step, but will you be able to offer appropriate support for those who aren't ok? How can you enable your members to talk to and support one another about distressing issues? Will you talk publicly about events that affect your members? These are all things that are worth considering before something happens, so that you are ready when it does.

Community goals

Mission/purpose change

Probably the biggest internal change that can impact your community is a change of mission or purpose.

WTS began with a focus specifically on women, because that is where I personally felt a lack of representation. Over the years, I came to understand that this lack of belonging in the industry didn't only affect people who identified as women, and I started working on ways to ensure that all people of marginalized genders would feel welcome in the community.

These changes included:

- Adding inclusive language guidelines to our code of conduct, The WTS Way
- Reworking our vision and mission
- Rebranding our community so that it is more inclusive for all people of marginalized genders

My work through WTS is one very specific example, but there are many ways that a mission or purpose can change over time. Perhaps your community began as a way for users of your product to provide feedback, but over time it has evolved into a space for them to connect and gather with one another. Or maybe you began with a platform to connect people from a specific industry or in a specific job function, but through conversations between members you uncovered a particular need or issue that you could support.

It is important to regularly refer back to the original mission and purpose that you defined for your community to check whether it is still relevant, and, if necessary, clearly set new objectives and goals.

It's also possible that the original purpose of the community no longer fits with your business objectives. If there is a change in strategy at a business level, Richard Millington recommends being proactive in your response to identify how you can adapt the community to these new needs and be a vocal spokesperson on behalf of the value of your community, before senior leaders decide the community is no longer necessary: 'Proactively identify the new goal; don't wait for it to trickle down (because those making decisions might preemptively decide the community doesn't match the new goal).'[2]

Teething pains

As a community grows, you might experience some issues with the way you initially set everything up. What worked for a tiny fledgling community might not suit a larger group. There might be too many conversations for you to keep track of, similar but disconnected conversations happening in different places or a lack of clarity on how the community can engage with you.

Continually reflecting on what's working and what isn't gives you opportunities to consider how you can adapt your setup for changing needs. Perhaps you need to categorize topics in a better way, or maybe there are ways to make the processes more efficient. You might need more moderators or new community rules. Keep checking in with your team and your members to identify where you can make improvements.

Stakeholders

Senior leaders

When the senior team in your business has been fully bought into the value of your community, changes to that team can lead to a certain level of uncertainty. Will the new leaders be as willing to support you as the previous ones?

As we saw above, being proactive in demonstrating the value of community to the wider business goals is important. Spending time getting to understand the priorities of these new members of the leadership team and showing how your community supports those can help in getting them on side, using any metrics you have to support the value of this work.

If the senior team have been heavily involved in the community, you will need to educate new members about how the process works and their role in it all, in a way that helps them to feel enthusiastic about it and bought into the vision.

As Richard Millington points out, changes to the senior leadership team might mean you need to agree on new objectives for your community, ensuring that these new objectives are achievable and valuable.[3] It might also mean adapting to changes in budget or resourcing. We've already looked at how you can manage changes in community objectives, and we'll look at changes in budget and resourcing shortly.

Team members

Over time it's likely that staff will leave and be replaced from your community team, and you may expand the team as the needs of your community increase.

Your new staff will bring different skills and perspectives that need to be taken into account, and which may influence the tactics you use. They will also need training and onboarding to enable them to understand your particular community and how it works, as well as closing any knowledge gaps. There might need to be reallocation of tasks or reviewing of role descriptions.

Diversifying your community

As your community grows, you are likely to end up with a more varied group of people who will have a broader range of interests and needs than those you initially started with. Keeping a dialogue open with your community to understand how you can best serve them will allow you to adapt effectively. You should keep reviewing the way your community works to identify any ways you can evolve to meet changing needs.

As your community diversifies, you may need to give more thought to moderation in order to maintain a safe space within your community and bring harmony to the group. Changes and additions to the code of conduct may also be useful, which need to be communicated clearly.

You may also need to consider, as your community grows, whether it isn't diversifying of its own accord. If your community is becoming quite a homogeneous space, you may want to take action to encourage greater diversity. This might mean collaborating with other communities to attract a wider range of people, or considering your approach to inclusion within your platform to make people from underrepresented groups feel more welcome, or looking at how you promote your community to see if you are inadvertently putting off certain people. Getting feedback from within your community, and also from other communities of people who are not represented within your membership, will be valuable in helping you identify any gaps.

Resources

Technology/platform changes

Most organizations rely on third-party platforms to host their communities, and this means that they are at the mercy of any changes made to these platforms which are out of their control. A provider might increase their prices, change their functionality or even cease to exist altogether.

Another way your approach to platforms can change is if you initially set up on multiple platforms and find later that you want to streamline your community or you find another solution that suits you much better.

These changes may mean you need to adapt the way your community works within your existing platform or change the platform you use altogether. It might be time to go back to the drawing board, in which case you can refer back to the guiding questions set out in Chapter 3 and reconsider your needs.

As you saw from my journey with platforms in Chapter 3, and you will see in many of the case studies within this book, it's normal for communities to need to adapt their platform use or change the platform they use over time. This is something you should be prepared for.

The same applies to your distribution channels. For the longest time, X, formerly known as Twitter, was the highest engaging social media channel for WTS. But in recent years, our primary audience has slowly been leaving the platform and spending more time on other social media channels. We knew we had to pivot and focus more of our efforts on other channels, and even joined new ones that we weren't previously a part of, such as Threads and TikTok.

When any part of your business is reliant on third-party tools, it's good to have a Plan B. Even when you think you've found the perfect platform and everything is going well, you should still keep an eye on what other options are out there and what new tools are being developed. It's also worth monitoring what other communities are doing with their platform so you know what else is possible.

If you do need or choose to migrate to another platform, communicating clearly with your members will be vital in helping them to understand and make the change, and then onboarding them to the new platform.

Financial changes

Most teams in most organizations have to deal with changes to their budgets at one time or another. It may be that, at one time, community was front of mind for your business and a lot of resource was dedicated to it. But then changes in organizational strategy or changes to the wider economy might mean there need to be team adjustments or budget cuts. You might find yourself running the community with reduced resources.

In this case, as Richard Millington points out, you will have to adjust your tactics: 'Prioritize tactics which have the most reach and depth. This usually means cutting out the least effective tactics and prioritizing the things that might have the most reach/depth/longevity.'[4]

In other words, you need to consider what's truly vital to your community, and what makes the most impact. You may have to let go of the rest. Use a grid similar to the one shown in Figure 10.1 to consider

Figure 10.1   Impact assessment

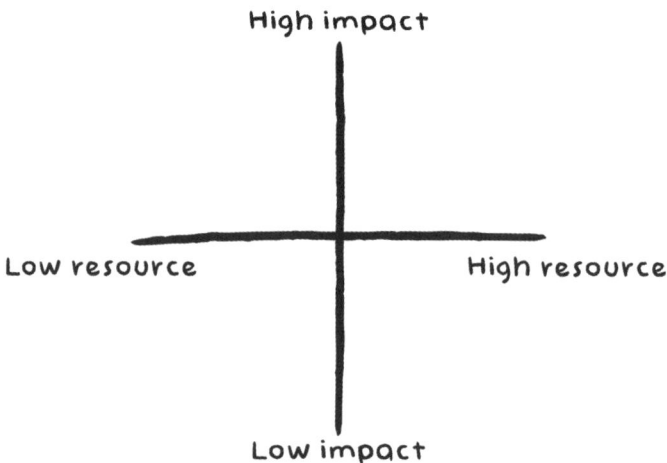

your current tactics in terms of the level of resourcing they require and the impact they have.

Anything in the 'low resource/high impact' section should be a priority, and elements in the 'high resource/high impact' should be considered in the context of your new situation. The elements in the 'low resource/low impact' are a much lower priority, and the elements in the 'high resource/low impact' section can be eliminated.

Communication is key

Whatever changes you come up against, communication is key to navigating them effectively.

You have a diverse group of members who have joined over different periods of time – some have been with you from the beginning, some may have only just discovered the group. The way they adapt to, and react to, any changes will be very different. Some may be enthusiastic, some decidedly opposed. You will need to talk to and engage all of these people, being mindful and supportive of their different views, to keep them on board.

Many communities make the mistake of trying to perform changes in the background hoping no one will notice. Your members will certainly notice, and they are likely to be more unsettled and displeased if they haven't been prepared. They will also want to understand why these changes have come about. Telling them in advance that changes will be coming, and why, will help them feel more comfortable and accepting.

You can also ask for feedback before you start rolling out any changes, perhaps by bringing together a focus group to discuss your proposed actions and asking how they feel about them. When you make your community part of the decision-making process, they feel valued and bought-in to a change they feel they've been part of.

There's only so much you can control

In the end, you need to focus on what you can control, accepting that those elements are limited, and let go of the things you can't control.

You may not be able to do much about fluctuating economies, shifting technologies or global conflicts, but you can control how you respond to those challenges, and how you communicate that response. Being prepared as much as possible will help you, not only by considering what changes you might face, but also by knowing what works well in your community and what it truly needs, so that you understand what needs to be prioritized during any period of change.

Taking learnings from any challenges you do encounter, and getting feedback from your community on how change has been managed, will help you to move forward with everyone feeling stronger and more connected.

In the next chapter, we'll work on putting our learnings down in the form of a long-term plan for sustaining our community.

Key takeaways

- There are four main types of change you are likely to face: changes in external factors, community goals, stakeholders or resources.

- External factors might include changes in your industry – such as a change in focus or a shift in the way a particular role works – or global factors, like conflicts and health emergencies.

- Changes to community goals might involve a shift in mission or purpose, or adapting to teething pains you experience as the group grows.

- Changes in stakeholders might mean personnel changes in your organization's senior leadership team or within your own community team, or a diversifying of the membership of your community.

- Resourcing changes might be brought about by new platform requirements – either by choice, because another platform would serve you better, or from necessity because your existing platform is no longer an option, or by financial constraints.

- Being prepared for the kinds of changes you might encounter and thinking about potential solutions will mean you are ready to adapt when necessary.

- Communication is key – keep your members informed, support them through the change and, if possible, involve them in the change in advance so that they are bought in.

Reflection questions

Here are some questions to help you prepare for change:

1 Where are you vulnerable to change? Are you reliant on third-party tools? Is there a particular member of the senior leadership team that champions community within the business? Make a list of all the changes that might be problematic for your community.

2 What will you do if those changes happen? For each one, make a list of possible responses.

3 What are the key priorities for your community – the tactics that make the most impact and the elements that your members value the most – that need to be protected during any change?

Notes

1 Feverbee. How to develop a community strategy, no date, www.feverbee.com/strategy/types-of-change/ (archived at https://perma.cc/8BT5-5HUK)

2 Feverbee. How to develop a community strategy, no date, www.feverbee.com/strategy/types-of-change/ (archived at https://perma.cc/8BT5-5HUK)

3 Feverbee. How to develop a community strategy, no date, www.feverbee.com/strategy/types-of-change/ (archived at https://perma.cc/8BT5-5HUK)

4 Feverbee. How to develop a community strategy, no date, www.feverbee.com/strategy/types-of-change/ (archived at https://perma.cc/8BT5-5HUK)

Building for the future   11

We've come a long way – we've gone from the first seeds of an idea to a thriving and engaged community that is growing and scaling.

Before we sit back and congratulate ourselves on a job well done, there's one last thing to cover – how will you define success for your community and plan for long-term growth based on those goals?

Where are you now?

This is a good opportunity to stop and reflect on how your community has progressed.

Consider how your community has evolved, and whether this is how you intended it to develop. If not, is that an issue that needs to be addressed or a positive new direction? Is your community meeting the needs of your business that you intended it to? Is it meeting other, unexpected ones? What has been working well? What's not been working so well? What opportunities are there for your community?

Given all of these factors, you can begin to plan your next steps and future strategy for the community, considering any changes in direction that you want to make.

This is also the time to reflect on the success of your community and measure your progress against your goals.

What success means to you

As we've discussed previously, 'success' means different things for different communities, depending on the needs of your business and your specific mission. Success is also rarely about the straightforward quantifiable metrics you might be used to.

Christina Garnett likens measuring the success of a community to that of social media. 'The fact that you start a brand account, you start a community, a lot of what you're looking at initially is vanity metrics. That's all there really is to go on. How many people are following us? As that brand account or that community matures, the KPIs look very different, because now you have people who are engaging with each other, and now they're talking to each other, and now there's events; what are the ripples that you're creating?'

Christina told me the story of two members of the HubSpot community who, having met through that community, are now starting a business together. 'They met each other because of this programme, and they got more opportunities because of it, and now they're working together. This is what community looks like when you do it well. Things are created that never existed before because of these connections that you're fostering and creating. It's really lovely to see.'

Coincidentally, something similar happened in the Women in Tech SEO (WTS) community: two members, Tory Gray and Sam Torres, met in the group and then co-founded a company together. When asked what I am most proud to have accomplished through WTS, it's stories like that which come to mind right away.

Alan Moir says that The TEFL Org have been impressed by the value in resource and connection that their community has given them: 'It can feed so much into other things, like updating the website, information that we might not have or is really difficult to source, and finding people or getting introduced to people that are on the ground and can help with that as well.'

Laura Roth agrees that these 'story wins' are an important part of measuring a community's success: 'That's the storytelling I try to combine with the data to tell the C-suite members because they won't know that. They won't even see it. It's not visible even if they're out there, but those stories are really powerful.'

Looking at success in this way requires a mindset shift from a quantitative to a more qualitative approach, thinking about the impact of the connections made and the strength of relationships formed. But this doesn't mean that there are no quantitative metrics.

We'll look in just a moment at the very tangible measures you can put in place, but, as Christina Garnett says, it's important to strike a balance: 'I find that especially in community, quantitative is important but it will never tell you the whole story, ever. You have to care about the qualitative.'

This balance between quantitative and qualitative is important, because you will need to highlight the story wins and experiential successes through the lens of what they are achieving for the business overall. Quantitative data provides a foundation to show the benefit of community, but qualitative data brings that narrative to life. As Pete Heslop, managing director of Steadfast Collective, says: 'Success for a community has to be aligned with the business objectives.'

Setting key performance indicators (KPIs)

If all this talk of stories and experiences feels overwhelming, never fear – you can absolutely set some specific, tangible and quantifiable metrics that will fit into a regular report. What these look like will depend on the needs of your business and the goals of your community.

Some KPIs you might measure include:

Community growth

- **Number of members:** how many people are in your community, and at what rate is this number increasing over time?
- **Number of initiatives:** how many new initiatives have been launched, and what was the engagement with these?
- **Number of events:** how many events have been held, and how many people attended?

Engagement

- **Number of engaged members:** how many members are interacting within the platform each week/month, and/or what is the engagement rate on posts/content you share? Some platforms (such as Slack) will tell you what percentage of your total members are actively engaged.

- **Retention rate:** how many members stay with you after six months/ one year? What percentage of your total membership leaves the community each month/quarter/year?

Customer service

- **Number of messages:** if one of the goals of your community is to provide customer support or to drive interest in your product, how many messages are you receiving through the platform from customers or potential customers?
- **Number of answered/unanswered questions:** how many support questions are answered within the community, and what percentage are answered within different timeframes? You could also compare this with a reduction in questions through other channels to see where your community has saved time and resources.

Monetization

- **Partners/sponsors:** how many do you have and how much revenue are you receiving from them?
- **Paid members:** if you have a freemium model, what percentage of your members are paying? How much revenue do you receive from paid members?
- **Renewal rate:** what percentage of paying members renew their membership?
- **Revenue:** what revenue/profit do you receive from paid events or other paid initiatives?

Distribution channels

- **Social media followers:** how many followers do you have on different platforms?
- **Email subscribers:** how many people are subscribing to your newsletter?

Simply recording these numbers is one thing, but you will also want to look at how they change on a monthly, quarterly and annual basis to assess whether your community is growing effectively.

You will also want to look at any links – does an increase in social media followers lead to an increase in community members? Do more engaged community members lead to more email sign-ups? Do more events improve your retention rate? There are lots of different metrics that can influence one another. You can also use your metrics to identify any seasonality trends and understand how best to adapt to these.

Joining the dots

Whatever measures you are using, the important thing is to understand the meaning behind them, and how they relate to wider business objectives.

At HubSpot, Christina says they are able to track both contribution towards their goals and mission, and financial benefits to the business. 'We look at engagement, we look at how many members are in there. We also look at how many problems were solved by the community instead of support, because that's hours saved, that's money saved. That's time that support can now focus on more intricate, harder level questions that maybe would've been bad enough that if they weren't solved, someone would've left. Now we're looking at retention, and more and more communities are becoming tied to retention.'

It's important to note that some metrics need both a quantitative measure and a qualitative view to ensure that the numbers are guiding us in the right direction. Christina gives the example of engagement: 'Let's say they are engaged, but what does that behaviour look like? Are they answering questions or are they just commenting? Are they giving us ideas or are they doing something else? Because you can say it's highly engaged but that could be because they're all yelling at you.'

Knut Melvær says that, at Sanity, they keep things simple with a few specific quantitative measures, and a qualitative overview of the health of the community. 'I'll look at how many weekly active people there are, at how many contributions there are, but it's more seeing the health of it rather than having explicit 'now we should grow this, this way and that way.' We look at how many sales conversations we have as a proxy to our revenue and then we see how many active users there are. Those are our North Star metrics.'

Laura Roth echoes the advice to keep it simple, and points out that it's easy to become overwhelmed by the amount of data that you can measure. 'With online communities, you've got the ability to measure a bit more. But you can measure too much, and people can get locked in and go down the rabbit hole a little bit. Keep it simple. Find a few metrics that align with your business goals for that quarter and work on that.'

Laura stresses that these metrics have to be closely aligned with the overall goals of the business. 'You've got to find what matters to the company. If you're doing an event, for example, the event space is so community-related, now more so than it ever was. I worked on an event for a former employer in the US, and that was a huge customer conference, and the focus was on, "How much more pipeline can I get in the room for sales?" The measures were: "Can we get X per cent more pipeline, and also increase the average customer value of the person in the room compared to the year before?" It builds back to the metrics that people at the top really care about.'

Setting targets

You don't want to be simply recording numbers, though. You need to set targets that align with your community goals and business objectives, and keep track of your progress so you can make adjustments to your strategy if needed.

Your targets should be SMAART:

- **Specific:** make the target clear, well-defined and easy to understand.
- **Measurable:** put quantifiable criteria in place to enable everyone to assess whether the target has been reached.
- **Achievable:** make sure the target is realistic and within your power to reach.
- **Assignable:** give someone responsibility for the target and ensure everyone knows who that person is.

- **Relevant:** the target should be aligned with your community and your business's overall mission and purpose.
- **Time-bound:** put in place a clear timeline for when the work should begin and the target should be reached.

Don't wait until you've missed a target to do something about it – if you are monitoring your data closely, you should know a reasonable amount of time in advance if you are unlikely to meet a target. In which case, you need to identify the reasons why you're falling short, and work towards addressing these.

Communicating with stakeholders

It's important that you keep all stakeholders updated on your plans, your targets and your progress.

Stakeholders might include:

- Team members of the department managing the community (e.g. the marketing team)
- Teams across the business who benefit from insights from the community
- Budget holders (e.g. finance department or CFO)
- Senior leadership team

Different stakeholders might want varying levels of detail and regularity in their updates, but these are some ways you can keep them informed, listed in order from most detail for those who need to stay closest to the community's performance to least detail for those who need only the big picture view:

- A dashboard of KPIs that is automatically updated and can be accessed at any time
- Weekly team check-ins
- Monthly or quarterly report on KPIs, including progress against targets

- Monthly or quarterly meetings on the performance of the community
- Quarterly or bi-annual meetings looking at community in relation to other channels (such as social, email and so on)

Investing in growth

Reporting on the numbers that the people at the top are interested in is what will help you secure ongoing investment. Christina, Laura and Knut all stressed the importance of ensuring that the senior leadership team are bought into the vision for the community, in order to secure long-term support for its growth.

This isn't a problem for Sanity, where the C-Suite are now fully convinced of the value of community – which makes Knut's job much easier: 'The CEO and the founders understand the importance of this. I don't have to defend it. That creates less pressure to come up with the numbers. It's not a very hard sell. It's more about the prioritization.'

Christina spoke above about the need to measure community membership's impact on customer retention, and this is tied to very real financial benefits for the business, which makes proving the business case for community much easier – there is a tangible return on investment: 'You're going to have to look at influenced MRR [monthly recurring revenue]. That tie has always been there. That KPI has always been there, but now it's the lifeblood. You have to prove the business case.'

Laura Roth has also found ways to tie community measures to very tangible financial returns. 'I always think an equation such as, a community member is X per cent more likely to renew or upsell or similar, and if that's much more likely versus a non-community member, that's gold dust. Or a connection to an NPS [net promoter score], the NPS of a community member is X per cent higher than the NPS of a non-community member. These things start to show the money and the value of it.'

Alan Moir also told me that the benefits their community at The TEFL Org has demonstrated have convinced department leads that community is where they should be focusing investment. They can see that what's been done so far has been worth it. 'With the amount of work that we've put into it, we've got a lot back, either through social listening or finding out what our students need and finding resources such as guests for their podcasts or being introduced to people. That's worked for us. We've got a lot of resources out of it. That leads to thinking, "Well, if we put even a tenth of that effort back into the community, imagine what we could get out of that as well".'

This willingness from the leadership team to invest is crucial, as you need ongoing commitment, budget and resource to be able to continue to scale your community and grow your efforts.

If you have that backing from above, then you can:

- **Grow the community team:** Be clear on what gaps need filling in the team, or what roles need further resources. For example, do you need someone to set the strategic direction for the community or an events specialist to build your events strategy, or do you need more moderators to keep track of posts or support team members to answer questions?

- **Develop initiatives:** This requires an understanding of what initiatives have been successful and what they have done for the community and the business, as well as what your members are looking for, so that you can predict what you need to develop more of and what results you can expect from doing so. As we saw in Chapter 5, diversifying your initiatives can be valuable for retaining members.

- **Create events:** As with initiatives, you will need to know what has been successful and what impact has been had, as well as what demand there is, so that you know where to invest more resources. Refer back to Chapter 6 to help you make plans for your events strategy.

Building a long-term plan

At the very beginning of this book, we looked at your vision and goals for your community. Now I want to close by ensuring that you have a long-term view for the future of how you can make those a reality.

This will involve taking everything you have learned so far, and everything you now know about your community and what works, or doesn't, for your business, and using it to guide your planning. So far together we have looked at:

- **Launching a community:** In section one, we discovered that there are many types of community and many forms they can take, but that community is, at its heart, about relationships. These relationships have to be reciprocal, and both you and your members need to be invested in that connection. We have seen the importance of having a clearly defined vision and mission that shape how your community is set up and run, and a framework for bringing these to life, all of which forms the basis for those human connections and attracts people to a space in which they can find people they want to connect with. Finally, we looked at how important it is to build structure and functionality with your audience in mind, and ensure the platform you use meets their, and your, needs.

- **Growing a community:** In the second section, we talked about the value of focusing on quality over quantity and building meaningful interactions. You know, now, how to make the customer journey as easy as possible, and how to build social proof that encourages new members to join. We discussed strategies for retaining members, and regularly reviewing feedback to make sure you are providing them with value. We prepared for challenges that might come our way, and put in place tools and processes to respond to issues.

- **Scaling a community:** In this third section, we have examined how to capture and action community insights, and the huge value these can provide to your business. We have looked at the benefits of partnerships and how to make these work effectively. You have defined success for your community and put in place the measures to help you understand whether you are achieving it.

Now you are ready to define your long-term plan. This should always go back to the 'why' we discussed right at the start of Chapter 1. It might be worth revisiting this question now, having learned so much since I first asked you the question: why do you want to build a community? Does your answer back then still apply, or has it changed?

You can also go back to the vision and mission you set in Chapter 2 and see if these still feel relevant or if some adjustments are needed. Then having considered what success looks like, you can build a plan from the top down that looks at goals for the following timeframes:

- 5 years
- 3 years
- 1 year
- Quarterly
- Monthly
- Weekly
- Daily

Start with the big five-year vision, then break it down into what you need to achieve in gradually decreasing timeframes in order to get there. That way you can draw a map from where you are now to where you want to be.

What comes next

I hope, by now, that you're feeling confident about what you want to achieve with your community, and how you'll know if you're on the right track. As we've seen in this section, your insights from your community will go a long way to telling you what you need to build to meet their needs, as well as what is working and what isn't, and how you can improve. The partnerships that you develop along the way will also provide you with valuable feedback and help you accelerate your growth. The key is, as we saw in this chapter, to know exactly what success looks like so you know when you achieve it – and if you don't, you'll know why and how to fix it.

In the next section, I have three detailed case studies to share with you, followed by learnings from a number of brilliant community leaders, to provide you with inspiration and guidance that you can apply to your own community.

Key takeaways

- Make sure you are taking time to reflect on how your community has evolved, as well as what's working well and what isn't.

- Be clear on what success means to you – what do you want your community to deliver for your business?

- Balance quantitative measures with qualitative ones.

- Set KPIs and targets so that you understand where your community is performing well and where it's falling short.

- Keep stakeholders informed about the community's progress, with the frequency and level of detail each group needs.

- Be clear on what investment you need for future growth and what impact that can create.

- Build a long-term plan that is informed by your 'why' and overall vision.

Reflection questions

This is a good point to reflect on what the future of your community looks like.

1 Has your community been meeting the objectives you set out at the beginning? Has it been meeting any unexpected ones?

2 What has been working well, and what hasn't worked so well?

3 Knowing what you know now, what would success look like over the next 12 months?

PART FOUR
Stories from community-first brands

The TEFL Org: 12
Connecting teachers around the world

As we saw in Chapter 8, your community is a rich source of insights that can guide your strategy and approach. The TEFL Org community is a great example of this, as its decision to build a community was shaped by listening to its customers' needs from the very beginning.

The TEFL Org is the market-leading provider of Teaching English as a Foreign Language (TEFL) courses, with courses in the UK, Ireland and online. They have trained thousands of English teachers who have gone on to teach globally, creating a network of more than 185,000 people all around the world. Turning this international group of alumni into a structured and engaged community is the work of Alan Moir and his team.

Alan Moir is the operations manager at The TEFL Org, which he joined in 2012. He creates and implements the company's sales, marketing and communication strategies, and builds partnerships with recruiters and language schools worldwide. After listening to customers' requests and questions, Alan realized The TEFL Org needed to develop a community platform.

I first met Alan at a number of industry conferences that we were both attending. In 2023, he joined a cohort of my online Community Building course, where I learned more about his work at The TEFL Org. When I came to write this book and wanted to demonstrate how powerful it can be to be guided by your customers, I knew I had to reach out to Alan and ask him to share his story.

Alan shared with me his journey and how much he learned along the way. In this chapter, you can discover how The TEFL Org recognized the need for a structured community, how they set about putting the mechanisms in place, and how they have adapted and continue to adapt as they gain more information about their members' needs.

How it all started

The TEFL Org has been providing TEFL courses since 2008. Having taught English themselves for many years in France and Greece, founders Jennifer MacKenzie and Joe Hallwood wanted to help others explore the possibilities that this qualification can unlock.

Students can choose to take a course in a classroom setting or online. When learning is happening in a classroom, interaction and relationship-building with fellow students are automatic. But what about in a purely virtual environment?

When people sign up for a course with The TEFL Org, they not only get access to all the course materials, but they are also given access to a forum where they can chat with other students. This forum offered some opportunities for connection, but was not managed as a structured community. There wasn't a dedicated person in charge of managing it on a day-to-day basis; it was mainly for course-specific queries.

Alan and his team recognized that online-only students might feel isolated on their learning journey, and they noted concerns from potential customers who were considering an online-only course but were worried about not being able to benefit from interacting with other students. They also saw that existing students were automatically reaching out for this kind of connection, with the forums full of questions such as, 'Was anyone in the Nottingham course this weekend? It would be great to catch up.'

People were already sharing their information at the end of a course as friendships and relationships evolved naturally. They wanted to keep in touch even though they only had a two- or three-day course together. That connection mattered to them – they wanted to know how each other got on after the course and find out about their plans as they evolved. They wanted to support each other and be supported as they embarked on the next phase of their journey and put their new qualification into action, many of them going to live and work in new, unfamiliar countries where they would benefit from making new friends.

The TEFL Org started noticing that students were creating their own groups through WhatsApp, Facebook and LinkedIn. Many people were searching online and asking questions about The TEFL Org courses and English as a Foreign Language (EFL) teaching through platforms like Reddit. They realized that if they created these kinds of groups themselves in an official capacity, they would be able to participate in the conversations, offering expert advice and guidance, responding to student needs and bringing everyone together so that requests and discussions were not fragmented, making it easier for students to find the connections they were looking for.

Furthermore, this would answer another issue that the team had become aware of. They knew that, with the course forum system, once students completed the course and no longer needed to regularly log in to the website, they stopped using the forum. The TEFL Org lost its connection with that student. However, social network groups exist on platforms that people access daily. These would enable people to stay connected with The TEFL Org for as long as they wish, access advice and support throughout their career as an EFL teacher, and share their own insights and experiences with others.

Alan and his team began envisioning a system that enabled peer learning, where students could discuss questions and challenges with both their tutor and other students, who could offer insights from their own experiences. A space where these conversations and opportunities for peer support and connection could continue long after students had qualified, maintaining a relationship between The TEFL Org and their alumni and providing students with an extensive international support network.

Creating a structure

When they started setting up formally, their first primary consideration was how to organize communications across their distribution channels. Alan and his team were very aware that they shouldn't be broadcasting to their community, simply putting messages out. And they didn't want it to be just the voices of The TEFL Org team. They didn't want to be talking 'at' their members. They wanted to drive discussions or spotlight conversations that were already happening to enable meaningful engagement and add value to their audience. To do that, they needed to know what their community wanted out of the group.

The team also recognized that it was essential to have clear rules in place from the beginning, with full, upfront transparency as to what the community is about and what kinds of conversations should be shared. Ultimately, what they were aiming to do was connect students, creating a space where they could find helpful resources, get their questions answered and feel supported, as well as potentially accessing opportunities for the future. Alan says that they defined the purpose of the community as a place for current students and course graduates to meet, discuss and share their learnings with one another.

This messaging is communicated in a number of ways:

- After webinars, they are reminded that they could keep the discussions going afterwards through the groups.
- During course enrolment in their welcome email, as well as when they finished the course in the congratulations email, they are reminded of the support available in the groups.
- For inquiries on webchat, over the telephone and email, they are reminded about the resources that can be found in the groups.

The next step in bringing this vision to life was to establish boundaries that would enable and protect the community's purpose. They set out rules reminding members to be kind and courteous, as members were at different stages of their teaching careers. General group discussions are welcome, but for specific course inquiries, contact their tutor directly. One of the guidelines is to make conversations public within the group and avoid privately messaging members. Keeping discussions open and in public allows everyone to benefit from shared questions and answers.

Alan also recognized that he needed to safeguard his team – staff joining a Facebook group would have to use their personal Facebook profiles to do so, which would mean that community members would be able to contact those personal accounts. To mitigate risks, they explained in their guidelines that group admins worked during their working hours and that admins aren't obliged to respond to messages outside of their usual workday.

The logistics of connecting

Once all the key structural elements had been finalized, Alan and his team moved on to the user journey and how new students would be introduced to the community. They needed to integrate the community messaging within the existing workflow – Alan explains how they went about this.

'When someone signs up for a course, they get their booking confirmation and a welcome email from their tutor. Then, they'll also get signposted to our Facebook and LinkedIn groups, with encouragement that it's a way to interact with other students on the course.

'It can feel spread out through the course forum, Facebook groups and LinkedIn groups; this continues to be a learning process. The main difference is that the course forum is for tutors to answer questions directly related to the course, and the social media groups are for more general and open questions that students can help each other answer. It could be a question like, "When's the best time to apply for jobs in South Korea?"'

It's essential for The TEFL Org that it doesn't seem like they've created these groups to sell to their students. Instead, it's about building relationships between students and the staff team. They are keen to show the faces behind the company; all the people featured in the course videos are actual members of the team that students can connect with.

The official community currently exists purely online, but Alan knows that students organize their own offline meetups. Everyday conversations in the groups will likely include someone asking who else is in their town or city and whether they would like to get together after school. Members want their connections and conversations to extend beyond the online world, and this is something that The TEFL Org would like to support. The team is looking into facilitating offline gatherings and is considering tools such as meetup.com to help them. They are also looking at what functionality on their current platforms, such as Facebook group chat, might do the job.

As of 2024, the official meetups remain virtual, with webinars and Q&As, but the team can see a need for people to connect in the real world.

Social listening

As discussed in Chapter 8, having a community is a great way to understand your audience's pain points by observing what issues regularly come up in discussions. For example, The TEFL Org has noted that a common concern for students, which is a regular topic of conversation in their groups, is how they can find their first job after completing a TEFL course. Alan and his team responded to this need by creating videos to answer this question and provide further guidance.

They regularly utilize some of the questions asked in the groups to develop and update their existing courses. Simply looking at people's concerns and pain points can help shape their curriculum. In addition, before releasing a new course, they provide access to the first unit or so to a section of community members and ask for feedback. This early user testing helps inform any necessary adjustments to the course design before it is released to the public.

Alan's team also runs annual graduate surveys to get feedback from students on their experience with The TEFL Org and their thoughts on existing and planned initiatives. This gives them a good indicator of what will work and what won't. Asking for input from community members provides a good sense check before pushing something new out to the broader audience.

What's next for The TEFL Org

The TEFL Org community has grown rapidly. According to Alan, 'As of 2024, across both Facebook and LinkedIn groups, we have approximately 11,500 members.'

Alan knows that the business fully believes in the value of community and that this is a major priority as they move forward, but more resources are needed. Firstly, the aim is to bring in people focused on community management who can fully own that strategy.

As we saw in Chapter 3, it can be easy to get fixated on the details, like choosing a platform or a name for your community, and let this absorb too much of your time. As The TEFL Org's example shows, it's crucial to remain focused on the purpose of your community and keep moving towards that. For Alan and his team, that purpose is to create a hub where people can connect and find the information they seek.

Alan knows they have only scratched the surface of what's possible, and the team is brimming with ideas for the future. The possibilities are expansive, and Alan is excited about what is to come.

Key takeaways

- Be aware of what your audience is looking for so that you can respond to their needs.
- Make sure you are clear on the purpose of your community, and stay focused on that.
- Consider how community management and onboarding will integrate with your existing systems and workflows.
- Listen to your community – track the conversations that are happening within the platform, and actively seek out input and feedback from your members in order to gain valuable insights that will help shape your products and services, as well as the future of your community.

Sanity: Creating a CMS loved by developers

Knut Melvær is the Head of Developer Community and Education at Sanity, which he joined in 2018. Sanity is a modern content management system (CMS), chosen by industry-leading companies like AT&T, Tata and Figma. This customizable platform for creating, organizing and publishing digital content allows developers to build content management interfaces that maximize their teams' efficiency and impact.

As a platform that is used by developers all around the world, Sanity has a significant, and rapidly growing, community of users. Knut is in charge of the team educating and engaging these developers through learning programmes, content, demos and certifications.

I found out about Sanity through my husband, who is a software engineer. He used Sanity to build his consultancy website and mentioned how active their developer community is. I then made the decision to migrate our Women in Tech SEO (WTS) website over to Sanity. I reached out to Knut and asked if he'd be interested in sharing the story behind Sanity's success with their community, and I'm so glad he said yes.

In this case study, you'll learn how Sanity chose its community platform, what moderation processes it put in place and how these supported its growth, and how it collects and uses customer insights to inform its product roadmap. Knut also explains how its ambassador programme has deepened relationships and expanded its reach and why they don't get too hung up on metrics and numbers.

How it all started

Sanity launched publicly in November 2017, and Knut joined the team in May 2018 as their first marketing hire and employee number 14 in the company. He got the job after writing a blog post[1] where he sang Sanity's praises; it turned out to be the job application he didn't plan for it to be.

His role has always been focused on developer marketing and education, and one of his first tasks was to create a community space to connect Sanity's users. As Slack is a group messaging platform commonly used by Sanity's audience in their workplaces, the team chose it to host their community, and, as of 2024, it continues to be their primary community space.

The initial purpose behind creating a community was to get feedback from developers trying it out – as Sanity was still a fairly new platform, getting their target audience to test out features gave them valuable information about how to develop their product and target their messaging, and allowed them to answer any questions that new users had so that they could improve their experience with the platform and encourage them to stay with Sanity for the long term. They knew Sanity was different from most CMSs, and needed users' help to ensure the platform met their needs and that the value would be clear to other prospective customers.

In the early stages, Knut and Sanity's co-founder Even Westvang had a vision of a community of practice. By creating a space where people could exchange experiences about using their platform, the Sanity team and their customers could all work together to make the system the best it could be and ensure that developers could use it to its full potential.

The community setup

Sanity deliberated for some time about where to set up the community. Back in 2018, they felt their options were limited. They considered Discord and Discourse, but these didn't feel suitable for what they wanted to build at the time. Slack felt intimate; it was real-time, and they felt that most of the people they wanted to reach were probably on Slack already, through work. This meant there would be little friction in their members' day-to-day lives between their work and their participation in the Sanity community. Slack was also how Sanity communicated internally as a team, so it felt very natural to build a community there.

Once it was set up, they started by informing their user base about the Slack community on their website and in onboarding emails. They ensured their customers knew they could come to the Slack group to ask any questions about the Sanity platform. They then created an automation so that whenever someone signs up for a new Sanity account, they are automatically sent a Slack invite. Knut and his team also realized they could design their backend system to retain all historical messages so that they could stay on the free Slack group.

The Sanity team introduced online meetups for the community very early on. One example was Open House, a virtual gathering for community members to connect and celebrate achievements. What made it special was that they had breakout rooms where attendees could hang out with different Sanity teams – just like at a physical open house in an office. Over time, this approach evolved to focus more on webinars.

In 2024, Knut and his team hosted several Sanity community meetups in Oslo, Berlin, London, New York City and Toronto.

Community growth

As of 2024, the Sanity community group has approximately 30,000 members, which is in line with their customer growth since anyone who creates an account is automatically added to the Slack community. The group mainly consists of developers, and one of the most popular and engaged channels is '#i-made-this', which gets weekly contributions from members promoting the work they're building. Because Sanity really understands their audience, they knew that their community would enjoy sharing and discussing their projects.

Knut hired their first community engineer in 2020 and, within a few years, promoted them to Director of Support Engineering. Many of the Sanity team are hired from among the community. Because members are so engaged with Sanity, they are eager to hear about and apply for opportunities, and Sanity knows that their members fully understand and appreciate their platform, making them great additions to the team.

Moderating the community

From the start, Knut was determined to build a space on the web that is centred on kindness, a place where people felt safe and welcome to ask questions. For a very long time, their tagline was 'There are no stupid questions.'

The primary way they set about creating that was to ensure that the Sanity team themselves modelled the behaviour they wanted to see. They are present and active within the community, and they demonstrate to members how to respond to questions in a positive way. They try to welcome everyone who joins the space as if they were arriving at a party. Knut wants people to feel that, as they come through the 'door', someone is there to say, 'Hey, nice to see you, welcome.' He told me, 'It makes the group feel more human.'

Moderation was also crucial. The group is predominantly moderated manually, although Sanity has used some of the automated features Slack offers. The built-in Slackbot can only send messages publicly to a channel, which is set to be triggered by certain events or keywords. Sanity has configured the Slackbot to remind members to use inclusive language. This involved a learning curve for the team, as their users are from all around the world, and cultural perspectives on language vary greatly.

New joiners to the community are also greeted by an automated welcome message, which shares the community code of conduct.[2] We touched on Sanity's code of conduct back in Chapter 2. The code of conduct lives on the Sanity website and includes the following:

- **Expected behaviour:** Some of the behaviours included are following the code of conduct, using inclusive language, being considerate of one another and celebrating each other.

- **Unacceptable behaviour:** This highlights that harassment is not tolerated and includes a list of what that may entail.

- **Consequences of unacceptable behaviour:** This explains that engaging in unacceptable behaviour may result in a warning and/or removal from the space.

- **Reporting:** This outlines how members can file a report if they have any problems.

Sanity shares reminders of this code of conduct with all members and makes public announcements to encourage members to be mindful of the way they treat one another.

Influencing the product roadmap

The community significantly influences the Sanity product roadmap. The insights it provides help Sanity understand its customers' needs, and members tell Sanity what's working well and what needs improving. Knut admits that, in the early days, community members spotted problems with Sanity's infrastructure before their internal monitoring systems.

This volume of data, in the form of feature requests and bug reports, generated by the community is highly valuable for the business but also challenging to capture and collate. Knut recognizes that they need to improve at this. The team is researching tools to help record and prioritize community insights, but they have yet to find the right one.

Another way that the community has been beneficial to the product roadmap is in user testing. When new features are in the alpha or beta stages of development, Sanity invites community members to try them out and provide early feedback. They sometimes offer company merchandise or gift cards as incentives to encourage participation, but often they find community members, because of their passion for the platform, are eager to try new features without needing incentives.

Community ambassadors

Sanity has been trialling a community ambassador programme, which they are looking to bring back soon. First, Knut says they want to consider how they can elevate their ambassadors, what incentives they can provide to reward them for their efforts and how they choose which stories to share. Currently, ambassadors are upgraded to Sanity's community plan, which offers more bandwidth and API requests, and they are given access to new features on the Sanity platform, which they can test before they are launched. In return for this, community ambassadors share their knowledge and insight from building with Sanity and help community members learn, collaborate and network.

Knut and his team are also considering introducing a referral programme to reward members for introducing new users to Sanity. However, this is still in the early stages of planning, and the technical elements have yet to be built.

Knut's philosophy is to trial out different ideas and see what works. By experimenting with different features and getting feedback from the community, he can see what is worth investing time and resources to take forward.

Sanity Exchange

There's the Slack group and all the conversations that happen there, but there's also the Sanity Exchange online hub,[3] where users can find all the guides, plugins and showcases for the Sanity platform.

Much of that content is user-generated because anyone with a Sanity account can log in to the community studio, add their resource and publish it on the Sanity page. Early on, Knut couldn't understand why anyone would want to do that. But he realized it's a perfect place for developers to display their skills and potentially attract referrals. Agencies and freelancers have shared that this channel is a vital source of new business leads for them.

Knut is keen to do more in that space to make it easier for people to contribute. This will also help their general users by giving them access to more guides and plugins and making their work more accessible.

What's next for Sanity

One of the things that most excites Knut about the future of his role is that he doesn't have to convince Sanity of the value of the work they're doing – he knows that the CEO and team leads understand its significance and are fully committed to supporting community growth.

This also means that Knut isn't under pressure to come up with numbers to justify his team's work, but they do track specific metrics to understand how the community is performing. The team measures overall growth and reviews the number of members active on the platform each week, as well as the volume of contributions to Sanity Exchange.

In the long term, Knut would like to explore the possibility of bringing the community to the infrastructure of the Sanity platform. It feels, to him, like unfulfilled potential to have the community exist separately from the product, and the high reliance on third-party tools, like Slack, concerns him. If the community was integrated within the product, this would add value to the members as they use the product, and the community could demonstrate to potential new users what could be done with the Sanity platform. In addition, as things stand, there are conversations happening and content being created across several different platforms, including Slack, GitHub, YouTube, X and more. It is a challenge to stay on top of all these platforms and ensure they're up to date. Bringing everything into a single space would make it far more manageable.

This vision may take a while to bring to reality, but Knut is excited about the prospect.

Key takeaways

- Choose a platform on which your team and your users are already active.
- Signpost your community as part of your customer onboarding process.
- Understand what your community members want and need to talk about and enable them to do so.
- Build relationships with your community members so that they are excited to engage with you and they want to contribute to your growth.
- Your team should model the behaviour that you want to see from members.
- Set clear rules and expectations around behaviour, and remind members of these regularly.
- Make good use of community insights, and consider how you will capture and use all the information you receive.
- Take a test and learn approach – experiment with new ideas and see what works for your organization and community.

Notes

1 K Melvær. Headless in love with Sanity, Medium, 14 November 2017, https://medium.com/hackernoon/headless-in-love-with-sanity-689960571dc (archived at https://perma.cc/K6BF-2ZLB)

2 Sanity. Community Code of Conduct, 2024, www.sanity.io/docs/community-code-of-conduct (archived at https://perma.cc/TJ5W-68NP)

3 Sanity. Exchange, no date, www.sanity.io/exchange (archived at https://perma.cc/F6HC-EY57)

Buffer: Building marketing tools with your customers 14

When I think of a community done right by brands, Buffer comes to mind immediately. I started using Buffer as a platform in 2013, and it was one of the first times I had seen a business building a thriving community for its customers. I was involved in their community ambassadors cohort in 2014 and learned a lot about their culture.

I knew that I had to include Buffer in this book, so I reached out to the Buffer team and asked if they'd like to chat with me about their journey with community. I was so pleased to get an email back from their founder, Joel Gascoigne, saying he'd happily talk to me himself.

Joel Gascoigne is the founder and CEO of Buffer, which was founded in 2010. Buffer makes social media and brand-building software for small businesses, creators and individuals. Their mission is to provide essential tools to help small businesses get off the ground and grow.

In this chapter, you'll learn how Buffer's interest in their customers as people and desire to perfect their product drove them to create a community, why they lost focus on that community, and how they rebuilt and reenergized those critical relationships with their members.

How it all started

As of 2024, Joel has been working on Buffer for the past 13 years. It's been quite a journey, and they've had different levels of attention to the community at various points.

During Buffer's first four years, there was a strong focus on community. Over the past two years, there has also been a strong focus on community. But what happened in between? There were strategic reasons why the team took their eyes off their community, and we'll explore those in a moment, but, ultimately, Joel looks back at that period with a bit of sadness because he believes they lost some of their strength during that time.

The initial focus on community in those early years goes back to the challenges Joel and his co-founder faced when they initially launched Buffer. As two relatively unknown entrepreneurs who were launching a startup that didn't have a known brand or reputation, they needed to build relationships to help amplify their product and attract new users.

Before co-founding Buffer, Joel had built and launched several projects in the past, but these hadn't worked out. He realized that his critical mistake had been not talking to his target audience so that he could understand their needs and validate what he was building. This time, he was determined to do things differently. It also fuels a drive to connect with people – thereby bringing together Buffer's first community – leading to a focus on transparency. Building relationships, having open conversations about people's needs and sharing information on what he was building showed Joel that open communication nurtured lasting connections with people who were then eager to champion his product.

Even before Buffer went live, Joel built a landing page where people could sign up to validate the need for the product. As soon as someone signed up through that page, Joel would email them personally to ask them questions about their needs and expectations from the product. He then kept in touch with these people, asking them for feedback along the way and providing them with progress updates.

Personal connections

In the first 12 months, the number of sign-ups was minimal. Joel felt it was crucial to get that type of insight, so he personally connected with each one through email and social media. He put time into understanding their work, their business and their individual use cases.

Joel remembers how one of the early Buffer customers was a photographer. Joel went through their portfolio and commented on photographs he liked. Those types of genuine connections made a difference, creating relationships with people who became loyal customers and enthusiastic brand advocates, as well as opening up honest conversations that would provide him with the feedback and insights vital for developing the product.

When Buffer was first launched, its features were limited. Initially, you could only schedule posts on X, formerly known as Twitter, and no other social media channels, and you couldn't post them immediately. You had to use a queue method and couldn't schedule for a specific time. The product's first version didn't even allow users to reset their password; people had to email Joel personally to do that.

In the early days, all customers started on a free plan, with the option to pay to upgrade. However, opting for the paid plan online didn't trigger the additional functionality – everything stayed the same from a technical perspective. Users could start recurring payments on PayPal, but the product didn't change, and they wouldn't even get a confirmation email. Joel would receive an email from PayPal telling him someone had upgraded, and then he would have to update the database manually and email the user himself.

Even though this was a platform limitation, these genuine emails formed a personal relationship with customers from the start. Joel felt intrigued and curious about every single person who used Buffer. People found this refreshing, and it helped Buffer connect with their customers.

These initial personal emails began a dedication to customer service that has continued as Buffer has grown. Joel always remembered how those early interactions fostered positive feelings towards the product in a new customer and enabled him to learn valuable information about them. Even though Buffer's onboarding is now a large operation handled by an entire team, they still look to connect with and understand each user.

Building in the open

As more people began paying for the platform, it became clear that this was a valuable product. This caused Joel to focus more attention on marketing so that more people would learn about Buffer. The team tried a few different marketing channels but landed on a community-focused approach.

At this point, in 2011, content marketing was reasonably new. Buffer created a blog to support their audience, who were also content creators, but they needed a way to drive traffic to it. They discovered that they could write for other people's blogs – also known as guest blogging – which would help raise their profile and enable them to link to their blog. Back then, blog comments were popular, and these were an excellent way to discover and learn more about your users.

Centring their marketing strategy on content enabled them to add meaningful value for their audience, and bring people together in a collaborative discussion about things that mattered to them – this is the essence of true community.

Buffer's commitment to transparency also served them well. It felt natural to be open about their progress and their journey – this is what is now known as 'building in public'. People found it interesting and exciting, and it opened up several new conversations, which allowed the team to see what types of people were interested in Buffer and how they gained value from being connected.

X, formerly known as Twitter, was also an essential tool for Buffer because it was public. As a team, they decided to respond quickly, accurately, and personally to any tweet they received, whether related to the product or not. That's where they started building their community, on X, in the open.

By 2012, they had put together a Slack community that could connect all their different customers and give them one place to talk to each other.

The 'middle' part

Joel always knew he wanted to have a freemium product that offered both free and paid plans – because it felt exciting to make it available to as many people as possible. The free plan enabled Buffer to acquire many more users quickly, as people were happy to try a product when they didn't have to pay for it. This made it easier to build a community, as new members were signing up on a daily basis.

But with a freemium product, once you reach a particular volume of users, it's relatively common to start thinking, 'Well, can we increase the conversion rate to the paid plans?' Joel admits that there came a time when their focus shifted to the paid product, and everything new they built was only available to premium users. They began to neglect the free plan and even found themselves questioning its value – it felt like a burden to provide high levels of support and customer service to large numbers of users who weren't making them any money.

They decided to shut down the free plan, and, at first, there was a substantial increase in users, as many customers upgraded to the paid plan to continue using the platform they had become reliant on. However, it soon became apparent that this uplift was short term. Once all their free users had either upgraded or left the platform, the team needed to actively recruit new users straight onto a paid plan. This required a sales-based approach, an entirely different type of business from the one they had started with. This was never the purpose behind Buffer.

Joel admits they lost the closeness of the relationships they had built with their customers during these middle years when the free plan was dissolved. When they launched new features, they didn't work closely with their customers anymore, and it no longer felt fluid or natural. Previously, when the community had been providing feedback on new initiatives and trialling new features, they felt like they were part of something, and they would be excited when these features launched. When Buffer put out an announcement, their community would share it far and wide to their own networks. When Buffer stopped involving their users in their development, this enthusiasm for and championing of the company dried up.

In late 2020, after the initial impact of the pandemic, Joel found himself stepping back. It also happened to be Buffer's 10th anniversary, and Joel took the time to reflect on why he started Buffer in the first place, who they were serving and what things were working for the business. The more he thought about it, the more Joel discovered a strong conviction that they should return to how it all started: reinstate the free plan, invest in it again and reenergize their community.

Having learned from everything that had happened over the last 10 years, the question was, how could they start strategically putting these pieces together as a more established company?

The right tool to use

The community is now hosted on Discord, and the Buffer team has been tightly connecting it with their product so that anyone in the community can opt into and enable beta features. It's an open community so anyone can join it, but they've been relatively deliberate about how people would discover it.

For several reasons, the team settled on using Discord as their primary community platform. First, many community members felt familiar with Discord as it is commonly used by other communities that their audience is likely to be members of. Buffer was keen to ensure the barrier to entry would be low and minimize any friction as much as possible, so they wanted to go with a platform their users already knew. The internal team also felt comfortable with Discord because it's similar to Slack in many ways. Secondly, they wanted to choose a platform where they could control and customize features. You can build on top of Discord through the Discord API, and Buffer found many ways to tie the community in with the product itself when some of these features are enabled.

When a new member joins the Buffer community, they're asked a few questions to understand what job role they do, and it then adds them to specific channels related to that role. This helps cluster the audience persona from the get-go. It becomes part of the community onboarding process. For example, when I joined their community space, I chose the small business owner option and was added to a channel with other small business owners I could connect with.

It's yet another way to recommit to a focus on bringing people together and getting them talking with each other about different challenges. That way, the conversations and the content that Buffer shares will be aligned with their customers' needs.

But, of course, the community is not confined to whatever platform is used. A community is a group of people interacting with one another, not the platform they're interacting on.

Buffer Suggestions

Buffer Suggestions is an open platform that the Buffer team created in 2023 for sharing a feature request or bug. Anyone can submit something, and it's fully transparent. The rest of the community can see all those submissions, and everyone can vote on which ones should be taken forward. The ones with the most votes rise to the top. It's a powerful way for the community to drive the product roadmap and strategy.

Buffer Suggestions is fully integrated with a user's Buffer account. Different people can add comments on the same feature request, creating a community atmosphere. The system is self-organizing because everyone can see and vote on the other suggestions. Buffer used to receive many duplicate requests – users asking for the same thing – but Buffer Suggestions has dramatically reduced duplication because people can see if someone has already put forward the same request and can add their support to that suggestion. It's also easy to merge requests, bringing duplicate or similar ones together, making it much more efficient.

It has the added benefit of keeping the team accountable because if something is at the top of the list, it's difficult to ignore it when it's open and transparent to the rest of the community. This incentivizes the team to respond quickly and prioritize work that the community needs.

If someone mentions a feature request in the Discord group that's already been added to the Buffer Suggestions platform, the team will send them a link and ask them to upvote it, but Discord makes it easier to discuss the suggestion in more detail.

They've also started directly integrating the most popular feature requests into the product, adding a Coming Soon section with options to be notified when a feature goes live. It makes the experience a lot more seamless, and users feel heard. Buffer Suggestions require some moderation in the background, such as cleaning out duplicate requests and consolidating similar features, but the Buffer team has product managers who look after that. Overall, it is a highly proactive way to handle feature requests.

Joel sees Buffer Suggestions as a lighter-weight, more accessible place to start with community involvement, and then Discord as the next investment step a user can take.

The community crew

The Buffer team doesn't have a dedicated community manager. This was a deliberate choice because they want the community to be a shared responsibility across the company. Joel believes that every role and function in the business can benefit from connecting with the community and understanding their actual customers.

However, to ensure that internal champions were driving the community forward, they formed The Community Crew, which includes people across all different teams. The Community Crew has around 10 members, including Joel himself, a product manager, a product designer, a customer support staff member and a few marketing team members. The group meets monthly to dig deep into community topics. Each of those people sees themselves as the connector between the community and their teams.

This means that community members get a much more targeted, better answer because the right person is responding to them. It also means that the internal team members at Buffer hear directly from their users. If they weren't having those discussions themselves, there would likely be a lot of aggregating of feedback, which might become diluted in the process. Hearing from customers directly is always more impactful than hearing information second-hand. A product manager or designer embedded in the community can also ask questions that a community manager may not necessarily think of, which could benefit the product development process.

Measuring success

Early on, Buffer's measure of success was community engagement – looking at how many conversations were taking place, and how many reactions and responses these were getting from people in the group. Once engagement had become strong, they focused more on the size of their community and scaling it up.

Buffer now feels their community thrives if members feel involved: their voices are heard and their input is valued. Measuring that isn't easy, but Buffer believes it's the most robust indication of success.

One example Joel uses in measuring success is that it's common for companies to offer vouchers to their users to get them involved in giving product feedback. But if you have a strong community and brand, you're committed to investing in that community and care about their involvement in the process. When you realize that you no longer need to offer a voucher to get community members involved in research because they already want to be involved, you know you have a successful community.

A thriving community is one where members want to impact the direction of the business and help shape the product – being able, as a team, to go in and gather insights from your customers without them expecting anything back. When it's time to launch the feature, those members cheer the team on and share it with their networks because they feel they are a part of this initiative and want to help it succeed.

What's next for Buffer

As of 2024, Buffer is in a rebuild phase. Joel feels like they've come full circle, and now their strategy and principles are rooted in their community as they were at the start. Joel describes it as, 'Just the day in, day out, chatting with people and connecting and cultivating it, just like you would with a garden.'

Joel describes reviving the community again as highly rewarding and exciting: 'It's inevitable that once you start connecting yourself with and building a community, you also receive it. You become part of something fun, and it makes work more enjoyable. Work feels easier because you have input from the community and customers. It's an overwhelming feeling.'

The Buffer team realizes that they will have to put the effort in. They will talk into the abyss for a while, even if people aren't responding to what they're saying. They just have to do it. It will feel uncomfortable, and the extra work will be challenging, but it's what needs to be done to reignite the community. It's all about pushing the boulder up the hill before it gains its momentum again.

Joel recognizes that this commitment to the community needs to be embedded within the culture of the business so that it is valued again. It's something they have begun to include in their hiring process, seeking to understand from their potential hires how they approach their online presence and community.

For Joel, there are two critical focuses for the future. One is embedding community and customers even more in Buffer. They don't want customers to feel like they're switching from one tool to another. Instead, they want the whole community and product experience to feel seamless. The second is helping community members connect. This can be done both online and offline. Facilitating and assisting connections between people feels like the thing that will provide the most value for their community members.

Joel wrapped up our conversation by saying, 'What feels most energizing is that choosing community first feels much more intentional this time. We've seen the value, and it's now intertwined with our overall strategy.'

Key takeaways

- Personal connections and interactions with customers build trust and loyalty.
- Being open and transparent about your growth and development helps your community to feel bought into the process and that it's something they are part of and care about.
- Don't assume that a community isn't providing you with value simply because it isn't directly making money – look at the broader benefits you gain from insights and relationships and how these contribute to overall business growth.
- Consider not only how you can build a relationship with your customers but also how you can help them build relationships with one another.
- Make sure that your commitment to the community is embedded in your company culture and that the community has spokespeople internally.
- Be willing to put in the hard work to build up a community – it won't happen overnight.
- Consider what success means to you – how will a community add meaningful value to your business, and how can you measure that?

Learnings from community leaders

In this section, 14 community leaders will describe in their own words how they went about launching, growing and scaling their communities and some of the key lessons they learned at each stage.

They highlight what went well, what didn't go so well, and any challenges they encountered along the way. They also share with us any lightbulb moments they had and if there was anything, in hindsight, they'd do differently in their journey as community leaders.

Amber Shand

Amber Shand is an award-winning software engineer, and the founder of She Bytes Back. She learned to code during the pandemic and has since gone on to dedicate her time to empowering women in tech to close the confidence gap.

The She Bytes Back community initially started as a newsletter called 'Imposter Methods' in September 2022 which gained traction very quickly. We had around 1,000 newsletter subscribers within a week of launching on LinkedIn. The primary content was around unpacking imposter syndrome as it was a huge issue facing women in tech. Each week, I'd share research and tips to help women in tech feel more confident in themselves, overcome imposter syndrome and feel more comfortable taking up space in a male-dominated industry.

The reason the LinkedIn newsletter did so well was that we created it just when LinkedIn had launched this newsletter feature, which meant that it alerted all 6,000+ followers I had and pushed a notification for them to subscribe. The great thing about LinkedIn newsletters is that they not only email all subscribers but also push out an alert to all your followers anytime you release a new edition – which is why it regularly gets over 60 per cent open rate.

However, to truly create a community, creating a standalone newsletter didn't feel like enough. I was still missing the connection between community members, and with it primarily being on LinkedIn, I got feedback from our members about not wanting to open up about the challenges they were facing on a public platform.

That led me to make a shift into doing virtual events in January 2024, and with this taking place in the first half of that year, I started seeing a decrease in engagement. From directly speaking to community members and through feedback forms, it turned out they wanted in-person events. I had to make a pivot – and I had to make a trade-off between building a community that was location-independent, to being location-dependent and based in London.

As a solopreneur in building up this community, in an ideal world, I would be doing both the virtual and in-person events – but managing time and energy while building a business and working full time, I must be focused on what will be the most impactful for my goals and will help the community thrive.

The lightbulb moment happened after our first in-person event in May 2024. We had a brilliant public speaking coach deliver a talk to the community about how to land paid speaking gigs. From the feedback, it was clear that the community wanted to learn more about confidence, public speaking and building a personal brand – but most importantly, they wanted to build up a powerful network of women in tech to lean on for support. Each event we have is shaped by the community from the data we collect from our feedback forms, and we use all information gathered from this to improve each event. Whether that's incorporating icebreaker questions and name tags, or giving them opportunities to practise their public speaking at an event.

I plan to focus on scaling our community and bringing in people to help, to alleviate my fear of failure when running events in new locations and the logistics of making it all work. The future of She

Bytes Back looks like bi-monthly events, annual conferences in multiple cities, and a resource and community hub for women in tech to connect, grow their skills and become the best version of themselves.

Briony Cullin

Briony Cullin is a digital marketing freelance consultant working with businesses across the world. Her specialty is SEO, and she provides training and strategy services. Her career path found her combining her love of food with marketing and community management.

I became a community manager by accident. I started food blogging when I moved to Scotland and inadvertently started growing a following on X, formerly known as Twitter, and Instagram. I loved the community side of social media and loved going to events where I met people in real life. I forged some really strong friendships from being chronically online in a country where I didn't know many people.

I was at a career crossroads when I saw a job advertised at Yelp, a user-reviews platform for local businesses. They were looking for a community manager for Glasgow. I loved Glasgow and loved raving about great local businesses, so the job appealed to me. Getting that job was a real highlight as it was such a liberating role with lots of freedom to write your own playbooks about building a community.

I took over an existing community, so there was a rocky period in the first six months. This was the most demanding period of the job because I had to make a lot of changes and encourage them to be more of a community rather than a clique. I felt like a diplomat trying to keep everyone happy but having one eye on the bigger picture of what the community should be like.

The role was quite unique as the community existed online, via the app and website, as well as in real life at regular events. As community managers, we aimed to get people to participate in the community and make the online space feel really vibrant – reviews of local businesses, photos, forum participation and more.

I did the role full time for over three years. It was less of a job and more of a lifestyle – the job was non-stop, and there weren't traditional working hours. We were expected to host events in the evenings and on weekends. Most of the time, I loved the social part of the job, but only towards the end did I realize how burnt out I was. I remember another community manager saying that she started the role as an extrovert and ended as an introvert. That resonated with me – it took its toll on me for a long time after the role ended.

Yelp decided to wind back its community manager programme and focus on the US, so they made all the international staff redundant. It was one of the best things that happened to me – I was ready to move on, and I was able to launch a freelance consultancy business that benefitted from all the connections I'd made.

This is probably my biggest takeaway from being a community manager and building a community: don't give the community all your energy. Keep some energy and time for yourself. It can be easy to get carried away when things are in a growth period – I got really addicted to the growth and the positive feedback I'd get from managers, as well as five-star reviews on my events. That fuelled me for a long time, and I just kept pushing that snowball up the hill. But it took away from other things I really loved – I stopped playing roller derby, cut back on cooking at home and spent a lot of time 'Yelping' when I could have been enjoying the holidays.

Having a community manager giving 110 per cent to a community is a positive thing. However, it takes away from ensuring that community members are connecting with each other and forging a community that is more than just one person. You can't be the only backbone of the community – that will stifle its growth in the long term. Build structures and strategies to allow your community to grow in a way that doesn't burn you out.

Dan White

Dan White launched the Digital Marketing Union (DMU) in 2019 as a deliberately small-scale, tight-knit online community for freelance and self-employed digital marketing professionals. With just under

100 members from around the world, it's a humble and private group of folks who share the stresses and successes of solo business.

The DMU was never intended to be a community. Initially, it started out as an online Slack for myself and a couple of other freelancers to hang out in. Self-employment is lonely, even at the best of times, so what we started with seemed like a good fit.

And fit is the word that I keep coming back to.

Communities can grow in so many different sizes and directions, and there is no right or wrong answer for the size and shape it should take. However, how you want it to fit – fit with your lifestyle, fit with your future direction, fit in with your other work is one of the most significant areas that I wish I had spent more time considering.

The components of a community are size, audience, revenue, resources and objectives. All of these parts have to align with one another in some way. If you want to be making vast amounts of revenue from subscriptions, then your audience could be small and paying a high price, or large and paying a low price (naturally, a large audience paying a high price would also be ideal), but does this work with your plans?

Or take your audience; if you only want to build a community for a niche that is so niche, would you have sufficient numbers for it to work? Or would your audience be so broad that really there isn't anything that unites or defines the people in the community?

Making a decision on any of these parts will then affect how the other parts of your community react – and how you intend to run things will need to adjust accordingly.

It's a hard thing to figure out. One which requires a lot of research, testing and refinement. And what you decide on will inevitably continue to adapt and evolve as months and years go by in the community.

With the DMU, I decided on a niche community; the maximum capacity I believe we'll ever have will likely be around 140 members. This is great because it keeps the community tight, and people know one another. It's what makes the DMU special. However, relying exclusively on subscriptions means that revenue from the community is ultimately capped unless we charge more per member. I could add more members, making it more mainstream, but then the DMU's tight-knit nature becomes increasingly diluted, taking away why people like the community in the first place.

In a similar but different way, the other primary consideration right now is the time the DMU takes up. Starting out, it was no more than one–two hours a week. Now it's one–two hours a day. And those one–two hours are split up into several chunks with multiple check-ins anywhere from 8 am–8 pm. It's a hungry beast.

In theory, this works fine, but friction starts to happen when we look at how it fits with the rest of my time. The other income streams I work on require deep work and several hours of uninterrupted concentration, making the two increasingly incompatible with one another.

There's no immediate solution, although there are options. It's a perfect example of finding something that fitted at first, but now the fit isn't working as well as it once did.

It will likely reach some kind of tipping point. Maybe going all in? Maybe hiring a community manager? There are definitely options, but figuring out what would be the best fit for both now and something that continues to work well in the future is what I'm trying to keep in mind.

Emilija Gjorgjevska

Emilija Gjorgjevska is a digital-native business engineer focused on user intents, lifelong learning, and self-improvement. Her expertise spans various industries: search, e-commerce, marketplaces, data, AI and entertainment. She is the founder of the Federal Committee of Designers of Macedonia.

Building and maintaining a community involves much more than simply forming a group; it demands dedication, expertise in the community's main focus, genuine care and offering unique value that sets it apart from similar groups.

I focused on identifying a strong product-market fit and favourable conditions when launching the community. There was a noticeable gap for a supportive community of professionals in the product, UX and UI design, where people could ask questions without fear of judgement. Prioritizing this unique feature during both the launch and growth phases, I provided value through free resources such as contests, job postings, industry news and upskilling courses. People were seeking a centralized hub to grow, network and learn for free, and I delivered precisely that.

However, challenges were inevitable. Adapting to various personality types was necessary as misconceptions arose about monetizing the group through hidden agendas. This misconception stemmed from the expectation that every community must monetize at every stage to make the investment worthwhile. In North Macedonia, providing something for free is unusual, leading to scepticism about my intentions. This scepticism even led tax authorities to join the group, threatening to investigate any monetization efforts. Despite these challenges, the community grew organically to over 4,000 members through cross-posting in other groups and word of mouth, as people recognized the effort, love and dedication I put into it.

Maintaining the highest level of community hygiene presented another challenge. While this is relatively easy at the beginning, it can gradually become difficult without proper processes in place. Initially, I established many rules and content moderation policies, which upset some members. People generally dislike strict rules; they prefer safe spaces and guidance that enrich the community and encourage positive contributions.

The importance of implementing effective processes to maintain community standards was a significant realization. Allowing people to argue or post irresponsibly is detrimental to the community. Introducing constraints, group rules and manifestos helps members align with the group's core principles. This approach attracts like-minded individuals who support the community through moderation and content creation.

Launching the community and getting it off the ground was particularly challenging. People research the background and expertise of a community leader; they don't automatically trust someone just because they've created a group. They want to see if the creator aligns with their expectations and values and, most importantly, if the creator is fair, transparent and genuinely inclusive. These qualities can't just be listed on a LinkedIn profile and expected to be believed. Proving your worth through actions, consistency and effort takes time.

Reflecting on the experience, I'd have introduced more moderators and content creators from the start, as multiple perspectives are more effective than one. Establishing more partnerships early on would have also been beneficial, as people frequently asked for recommendations on the best mentorship programmes or books to improve their skills in various areas. Being more transparent about my vision for the group and communicating it in a more approachable manner would have helped. People are more likely to follow community leaders who listen to them rather than managers who simply state rules.

Esme Verity

Esme Verity has worked in social finance and impact investing for over 10 years. She is the CEO and founder of Considered Capital, an educational platform with a mission to help impact entrepreneurs access the right capital.

In March 2023, I started a newsletter that would eventually become the business I run now, Considered Capital. We started with a handful of subscribers, and three years later, we're a community of 20,000 strong, 70 per cent female members, and changing the face of funding globally. I got to work building what I wanted to see and quickly realized that others did, too.

Getting anything off the ground is hugely challenging. It's only worth it if what you're doing is really important. To me, our mission is just that. Considered Capital connects founders and social entrepreneurs with the right sources of funding and support so they can free up their time and focus on building their businesses. It's a place I wish I had when I started my first business back in 2012.

Before I became a community organizer, I always believed that communities formed naturally. After stewarding communities for the last five years, I see now that effective communities require more than that. A community needs to have a reason to exist and somewhere for people to gather. This is the core of building a community.

My first role as a community organizer taught me so much about what I know about community. It was March 2020, the start of the global pandemic. The world was closing down, and people were craving online connection, community and support. I was running a community for purpose-driven founders and made two important decisions leading to a thriving community. First, even though it was a free community, I asked everyone to complete an application form before joining. This was an instant signal to new sign-ups that they'd be joining a curated, thoughtful community of like-minded people. Second, I arranged one-to-one calls with all new sign-ups to learn more about their businesses and what value they could add to this community. This one move changed everything.

These two actions were the most important things I did, and I have carried them through to Considered Capital. With a singular focus – funding – it was much easier to gather people and make it very clear what they were gathering for. Before Considered Capital, there was no business at all doing what I was doing. So, from day one, I was obsessed with creating the best community I could. I wanted a community space that went beyond 'inspiration' and gave practical and actionable support for time-short founders. Real funding opportunities, tangible case studies and practical tips for fundraising.

The goal was not to grow fast but to add real value and support founders to feel more confident and think outside the box when going after what they needed to build a successful business.

Looking back three years in, it amazes me how much support we've received from our community. We receive messages daily telling us how much confidence we've given them to pursue entrepreneurship and build a mission-aligned business. I heard many people say they would have given up pursuing this path if it wasn't for us.

Moving slowly, listening, and building with care and kindness do work. We hope to be part of a new wave of businesses choosing to do just this.

Fab Giovanetti

Fab Giovanetti is an award-winning author, entrepreneur and mar-keter of 15 years. She is the CEO of Alt Marketing School, which aims to make marketing more impactful, accessible, inclusive and fun.

Building a community isn't new to me. My previous business, Creative Impact, was a community for over seven years. I love communities, but they are hard work. So I said to myself, 'Never again', and yet there I was, starting another community, once again, three years later.

But, and that's a big but, when I launched the student community for Alt Marketing School, I knew I wanted to do things differently this time around.

This time, I wanted to create a safe space where students could ask questions, share their progress and really get stuck in their studies. I was still rooting it in belonging, but it was less about networking networking – it was about accountability and genuine support.

We wanted to redefine what a successful community looks like. We were looking at smaller numbers but a higher feeling of accountabil-ity. For us, success meant seeing students actively submitting their work, supporting each other and feeling like they could always come to us with their questions.

One thing that went really well during the launch was the social proof we already had. Our early members were graduates from our certification programme, so there was already a solid foundation when we opened up the community to the public.

As founding members, they got lifetime access to the community, so in turn, we noticed that, over time, not everyone was as active as we'd hoped. This is not to say that free communities cannot and do not work, but from our experience and our own community intent, we noticed that we needed a different type of investment.

Nevertheless, I persevered – I am nothing but stubborn! I went all in on creating more channels and encouraging more conversations, thinking that's what would bring the community to life. Spoiler alert: it wasn't.

After running an in-depth survey nine months in, I realized our messaging was off. Students didn't want more channels – they wanted a focused space to learn, ask questions and share their work without feeling overwhelmed. Looking back, I wish I'd treated the launch more like an experiment, testing different approaches rather than locking in on one strategy that took us a few months to adjust.

They say you teach what you need to learn the most. Funnily enough, despite my seven years of community design experience, I seemed to repeat the mistakes I'd tell clients and students to avoid. Even worse, I did not learn from our launch. As we grew, I still struggled to balance the type of content we thought our community needed with what they actually wanted.

At first, we kept adding more events, assuming more was going to provide more value. However, another survey revealed that our students actually craved more self-paced learning. They didn't want to jam-pack their already busy schedules with more events – they wanted to fit learning into their lives on their own terms.

This was a huge 'aha!' moment. We cut down on live events and shifted our focus to creating content that students could access whenever it suited them.

This change also freed us up to give more personalized support, like reaching out to students who were struggling to complete their courses. Little shift – huge benefits. Our students were shocked and, at first, sceptical that real people were reaching out to them. That shift was a game-changer and really reinforced the power of listening to our community.

Scaling is still a bit of a puzzle for us, but we're getting there. Early on, I realized that scaling wasn't just about getting more people into the community. It was about growing in a way that made sense for us and our members.

We are now involving our members in surveys to help us choose our subsequent releases, upcoming self-paced workshops, or even template drops. Little 'build-in public' moments for us. We are also sharing more vocal changes in the community – from feature releases to new shifts in the platform. You'd be surprised how excited your members can get when they learn they can send voice messages!

Our next step is to involve our members more deeply, giving them roles as moderators and coaches. This keeps the community active, and members engaged long after they've finished their courses. It's about making sure they feel like their journey with us isn't over – they're still part of something bigger.

Growing the community was hands down the toughest of all the stages. The challenge wasn't just about managing the community itself – it was about figuring out how the community fits into the bigger picture of our business.

I didn't have that clarity at first, and it made it harder to ask the right questions and give our members exactly what they needed. But, like everything, it's been a learning process. Building a community is about aligning that piece of your business with overall values and mission and how that community supports and aligns with the business's larger goals.

Looking back, the biggest takeaway for me is the importance of staying flexible and open to change. There will always be challenges, but if you're willing to listen, adapt and keep the needs of your community front and centre, you can create something truly impactful.

If I could do it all over again, I'd focus more on experimenting and personalizing from the get-go, ensuring every move we make is in sync with our community's needs and our broader business goals. But then, I am a curious bean by nature. Like I say to my students all the time, we never stop learning because practice makes progress!

Jack Chambers-Ward

Jack Chambers-Ward is the Marketing & Partnerships Manager at Candour, a full-service digital agency. As part of his role at Candour, Jack organizes SearchNorwich, a free marketing event that occurs every other month. He also co-founded the Neurodivergents in SEO community in 2023.

Both SearchNorwich and Neurodivergents in SEO communities are very different. The primary channel for Neurodivergents in SEO is a Slack group with members from around the world, and SearchNorwich is a series of in-person events that happen six times a year.

SearchNorwich returned in 2023 after a hiatus during the Covid-19 pandemic. The creators behind SearchNorwich had seen some other marketing events starting up in the area and realized that there was a demand for events catering to the search marketing community in Norfolk for the first time in over three years.

In a way, the origin story for Neurodivergents in SEO is similar, driven mainly by unanswered demands in the community. My co-founder and I had been discussing some issues we had experienced and how little support there is for neurodivergent people in the marketing industry. That was the spark that inspired us to create our own community for fellow neurodivergent marketers. We realized that no one else was going to provide a safe space for us; we would have to do it ourselves.

For Neurodivergents in SEO, the difficulty of balancing the growth of a community, our full-time jobs and families is only exacerbated by the additional day-to-day strain experienced by neurodivergent people. Finding the time to contact sponsors and acquire funding is a time-consuming task for anyone. We found that offering specifics for sponsorships, such as a webinar series, has been more successful than a broader and more vague community partner sponsorship. Of course, planning these events takes more time, so we decided to get some help from our community members to form a committee to drive the focus and direction of the group forward.

After that, the most challenging thing has been some of the friction we've experienced in the community. Sarah and I did not have any training with regard to conflict resolution, so when there were issues between community members, we found ourselves stepping into situations we were not prepared for. I'm very aware that conflict and issues between members are common in any community, and this is especially true when bringing neurodivergent people together with very different communication styles. We reached a resolution quickly, but I think we could have handled these conflicts better. We should have spent more time trying to understand the different perspectives to ensure both sides felt heard and understood.

SearchNorwich has been quite the opposite experience. We were able to secure a year's worth of sponsorship quite quickly, and there have been no issues with the attendees. The most challenging part has been trying to determine which marketing channels help drive ticket sales. When tickets launch for our next event, we typically sell

30–40 per cent of tickets within the first few hours. This first batch of tickets is from our returning attendees and advocates, a very important part of any community. The following 60–70 per cent of ticket sales is a much slower process.

The second wave of tickets usually sells when we announce our speakers a few weeks after launch. Then, there will mostly be a trickle of ticket sales over the coming weeks leading up to the event. Sometimes, a newsletter or social media post will convert well and sell some tickets, but it's rarely consistent or repeatable. Thankfully, through word of mouth driven by the organizing team and our advocates, we manage to reach 90–100 per cent ticket sales for each event. It can be challenging to balance a consistent strategy of emails and social media posts with liaising with various suppliers and speakers.

Both communities take a lot of work to maintain and grow, but the passion and feedback from community members keep me striving to do better and aim higher in the future. The Neurodivergents in SEO community has grown throughout 2024, with more than 250 members in the Slack channel and over 1,000 followers on social media within the first year. SearchNorwich will soon reach its 20th event at the start of 2025 with discussions of expanding to an all-day conference-style event in the near future.

Jo Juliana Turnbull

Jo Juliana Turnbull is the founder of Turn Global, a remote digital marketing consultancy, and the founder of Search London, a community of events for marketers in search.

Search London started in October 2010 when I took over a meetup group that had been running for those in SEO, PPC and social media. I had been looking for a safe space or a community where I could learn from others in our industry. I was leading the SEO team at a media agency and looking for peer support elsewhere.

I took over the group in October 2010, renamed it Search London, and then we launched our first event in January 2011.

When Search London began, it grew organically without a lot of promotion, and it went really well. We had events every six to eight weeks in central London, and we regularly had around 40 people attend each one. Most events/conferences at the time asked for experienced speakers, but I wanted a place where new speakers could present for the first time. I also wanted speakers from different backgrounds, not just from large brands or well-known universities. Everyone was really accepting and welcoming of first-time speakers, and we received a lot of positive feedback from the events.

One element that did not go well was that when we ran the events for free without charging an entrance fee, we had a lot of no-shows. Sometimes, we had more than 50 per cent of people not turn up, which made it challenging to preorder food/drinks and organize the venue. So, in 2015, I started charging for events, and people bought tickets on Eventbrite. Now, most people who buy tickets attend. Recently, we've found almost no dropouts for our events. Everyone who purchases a ticket is more likely to attend the event.

One of the unexpected issues was securing sponsors. It was easier to have space in a company's office that could host us, but it was more challenging to have companies put a tab behind the bar if we hired a private room in a pub. Over the years, securing private venues has become more complex as minimum spending has increased considerably post-Covid-19, especially for co-working spaces.

Some of the lightbulb moments were selling out of tickets without sending out emails. Very often, people see the promotion on social media, or we contact people we know, and they purchase tickets. People especially loved topics around technical SEO and 'how to', so we tried to focus on those presentations.

A genuine surprise was that I met so many supportive people and grew my connections through the community, some of whom became my friends. Search London led me to discover other communities such as Women in Tech SEO, The DMU, The Freelance Coalition for Developing Countries and Search 'n Stuff.

If I start the beginning part over again, I would set a plan in place to have more support earlier on. Ideally, I would want to pay people for their time, so I would make Search London a business from the start.

I would also focus on setting up a private community on a platform such as Facebook Group or similar. When I began Search London, I was conscious of not excluding anybody, so I did not build a private community group. I could have set up the email database from the beginning, but as we sold many tickets through word of mouth or from social media, I did not focus on this. We have since built up a following on social media and a good-sized database, and our open email rate for those attending our events is very high.

We grew relatively quickly and easily. However, sometimes it has been challenging to keep the momentum going, especially after Covid-19. There are a lot of other events out there, and as more people work from home, not everyone is in London. London has also become more expensive, so travelling to London just for the evening can be costly both financially and in terms of time. Many people have moved further out of London during lockdown.

However, many people are still interested in attending the online edition and the in-person events in London if enough notice is given. The digital community in Barcelona has grown considerably since I moved there, and so in June 2023, I launched the first Search London, Barcelona edition. We also had our first Search Barcelona dinner in August 2024, which was a success.

We will now look to host a number of different events, including online and in-person events in London and Barcelona, as well as networking events, workshops and dinners. We are constantly growing and welcome those who are in digital marketing to join us.

Jo Walters

Jo Walters works on communications and marketing consultancy, training and delivery projects with small organizations that are doing great things. She is the founder of 25 Dots and has worked extensively with student union communities.

Students' unions in the UK do great things. They're attached to universities and colleges, and they run things like sports clubs, advice services, shops, events and plenty more. They're democrat-ically run and generally have really progressive values. They're amazing. They're also chaotic, usually run on a shoestring budget, and their membership changes every year as students join and leave their institutions.

This means it can be pretty tough if you're tasked with commu-nicating everything the union does to a set (but changing) list of people with a range of interests and opinions. When I found my-self in this position, I wanted to learn as much as possible, so I went to some conferences and read many books. The students' union sector is very collaborative and happy to share ideas and resources, but I was after things specifically related to marketing to students.

I couldn't find anything aimed at people like me, so I thought I'd make it myself, as Areej has done with Women in Tech SEO. I booked a room, asked some interesting people if they'd share what they'd been doing and pulled together a really informal conference with around 30 people from a bunch of different students' unions.

At this point, I had no intention of creating a community, presum-ing this would be a one-off event or an annual event with no continu-ity or interaction between events.

A few years later, the conference had tripled in size but kept to its bare DIY roots. I love learning from other people, but it turns out I don't love running events!

People like me relished the opportunity to chat with other people facing similar challenges and learn from each other's great ideas (and mistakes). Plus, who doesn't love eating a massive pastry on a day out of the office?!

We stayed in touch in a very ad hoc fashion via email between events, and gradually, people built connections at the event.

One of the most touching moments was the year when I was preparing for the conference but was ill and was worried I wouldn't be able to actually run the conference. When I told the community, some of them stepped forward to finish planning it and deliver it on the day. It was so heartwarming to see that they were prepared to take it on so that people could still come to-gether to share and learn.

Primarily, switching away from email to WhatsApp made it easier for people to be in touch between conferences. The more immediate and informal channel means people feel able to ping a random question out to the group without having to put together an email and send it to hundreds of faceless people.

The conference has morphed into a new form, where other people are in charge of running the actual event, and people still find inspiration and solidarity by hearing from people doing similar work.

My community isn't a formal or even particularly active community. I don't even know if the people in it realize that I see it as a community, but I know they feel they belong and learn from the people in it. Communities come in different forms, all with their own advantages and disadvantages, and it's liberating to know we can just do what works for us and not panic about trying to build something massive or replicate a particular format.

Our community was created accidentally. I'm a very nosey person and love finding out what other people are doing and how things work. I wanted to hear from some smart people and thought it'd be weird if I were the only person in their talk, so I invited other people, and it grew from there.

On paper, I'd be the worst person to create a community: I'm an introvert who is socially awkward with people I don't know. I'm not great at following through on big long-term projects, but I'm also a control freak who hates to delegate. Sometimes, I wonder if I should've set up the community more formally and intentionally with a proper joining process and more structured projects and initiatives, but I think this is working fine for us at the moment. Perhaps communities reflect the people who start and run them, and I'm in my casual and slightly chaotic era.

I think it shows that if there is a group of people with shared interests and/or challenges, then great things can happen when they come together, and you don't always need a big plan if you have nice people doing incredible things.

Julia Bocchese

Julia Bocchese is an SEO and Pinterest consultant for creative small businesses at Julia Renee Consulting. Her goal is to make SEO and Pinterest strategies approachable and easy to implement for all small businesses so they can reach their ideal clients organically. She is the founder of a local community, the Philly Female Entrepreneur Coffee Meetup.

I am awful at networking in traditional networking settings. I know a lot of people say that, but I had someone come to my rescue at my first networking event out of college because I got backed into a corner and must have looked so out of place.

So, a few years ago, I decided to create my own community to connect with people in a way I actually enjoy and am comfortable with! I started a monthly coffee meetup for female entrepreneurs in Philadelphia and wanted to keep it casual.

I had been in some small online community groups that I enjoyed, but I wanted to meet more people in person without attending the typical networking events with people in suits. As an introvert, I found that large settings with everyone just making small talk are more stressful than beneficial for making meaningful connections. So, I started the meetup group, which is small and intimate, with up to 10 people joining each month. It's just a chance for people to chat about various business topics over coffee. Nothing formal and very low pressure.

There haven't been specific points that have been more challenging than others; we've just had a few ongoing problems. Since it is just a casual meetup group without membership fees or anything, it can be hard to get people to commit to showing up sometimes (especially in the summer).

We've also run into issues with finding coffee shops that are big enough for up to 10 people to sit together since many coffee shops in Center City Philly can't even seat 10 people in the whole space. We've had to hop around to a few places over the years because places closed during the pandemic or moved to another part of the city where it wasn't convenient for people to get to anymore. It has been a surprisingly frequent problem, and we've had to frequently find a new spot to host us.

But even if it's a little challenging to get people to commit to coming to meetups or finding places that are big enough, I wouldn't change a thing! I haven't seen a similar type of group in our area that's intimate, specific for women, open to any industry and free.

Since it's so casual and there aren't any formal agendas or high-pressure networking, I've found that it's easier for new people to feel comfortable coming and joining the conversation (especially fellow introverts!).

Since it's open to entrepreneurs of any industry, it keeps the discussions exciting and offers lots of different perspectives. We have people in the group varying from wedding photographers to financial experts, and I love all the unique perspectives everyone has to offer!

Penni Pickering

Penni Pickering has been self-employed for seven years, running a design studio with her wife, Jo. As a small team of two, they craved more in-person time with other freelancers and self-employed folks, so they created their very own community: CoWork Crew. They are currently opening up co-working days across the UK to bring freelancers & micro business owners together.

My number one tip for anyone about to launch anything, and one I thought I knew better myself – trademark that name. Long before it is thriving!

My wife Jo and I had been self-employed for seven years, and community is what kept us doing it. Freelance friends, co-working spaces, meetups in the evening. All of it. I had this nagging idea that there was room for a relaxed, friendly, local-first community for self-employed people. Those working from home or a coffee shop can get isolated.

We moved really quickly from idea to launch. The idea popped up in January, and in May, we were running our first event, local to us in Northampton.

Our unexpected problem? The name we chose, built a brand on and got people engaged with – someone else trademarked it between us checking in January and checking again in August. We'd chosen to wait to see if this 'idea' turned into something. And when it did, it was too late. So, we had to embrace a rebrand.

We're in month eight since deciding to go for it, so I've little advice on scaling, as we've got that journey ahead of us. But the launch is very fresh and ongoing.

The biggest thing I've realized is when a community does start to grow, it won't wait for you to catch up. At first, it felt really manageable, running one event a month locally. Then we spotted a want to keep up with each other between events. So, a Slack channel came along. And then there was a newsletter. And social media channels. And new community members with ideas and speakers to book.

A couple of months later, we started chatting with people who wanted to host the event locally in their towns and cities. All of this is incredibly exciting. And we're really excited to do it. But it has gone from pushing a ball uphill to chasing it downhill. Our community has grown, and now we need to keep up.

For us, at least, growing a community is effort first and earnings second. Every pound earned from ticket sales and sponsorship is reinvested to help us better serve the community and do more things for them.

That means we're increasingly working extra hours to support the community as it grows. While running our business, we need to keep paying the mortgage. We need to be careful about burnout.

An early lightbulb moment for us was a chat with our very lovely and trusted accountant. We asked for her advice before we launched, and I'm so glad we did. Most who choose to launch some kind of community are in it for altruistic reasons. I wanted to do this thing because I could see it doing good. That meant my thought process at first was to just do the thing for free. And worry about monetizing it later if it is successful. Luckily, I had that chat with my accountant. She stopped me from running away with doing it for free. Her advice? If I launched this community and people found value in it, I was doing them a disservice by not making sure it could pay for itself.

Ultimately, that would lead to either not doing as much as we could for community members or, worse still, having to stop because we weren't getting paid and, therefore, couldn't put in the hours needed to support it. Thanks to that advice, we did some forecasting and worked out a point at which we'd be happy to take a small salary. It isn't from day one, but that felt right for us. If the community grows to that point we've decided on, I'll feel justified in taking that salary. I feel I'm providing enough value to community members to qualify to earn an income from it.

Deciding to start a community was a terrifying step. It felt like leaping into self-employment all over again. What if nobody joined? What if we got it wrong? Eight months in, with a budding community of lovely self-employed folk doing better because they have each other, I'm so glad we were brave enough to try.

My advice to anyone who has that niggling feeling that there's a need for a community they've thought of would be to just try it. Keep the reasons it provides value front and centre, and give it a go. I think it is always better to try and fail than to always wonder 'what if'.

Ruth Cheesley

Ruth Cheesley is an Open Source advocate with over 18 years of experience using and contributing to many different projects. Having served on the Joomla Community Leadership Team project and built a full-service digital agency, she now works as Project Lead for Mautic, supporting the community that builds and maintains the world's first open-source marketing automation platform.

When we started to formally grow the Mautic community back in 2019 after growing organically since 2015, we faced a significant challenge: there wasn't really much in the way of a community culture. People would tend to drop in and drop out when they needed something – or to complain – but not much kept them engaged. This lack of engagement stemmed from not having clearly defined expectations for behaviour, contributions and values within the community. I realized quickly that if we wanted to grow our community sustainably, it would be really important to establish a transparent culture right from the start.

My vision for our community was to create a place where people helped each other succeed. A place where people were kind to each other, showed appreciation freely, and, most importantly, stayed around to help others. Kindness and generosity are the 'golden thread' that runs through our community.

We approached that in a few different ways – of course, there's the policy approach of developing a very clear Code of Conduct and accompanying policy of how breaches are dealt with, and tools such as AllyBot, which can be integrated into your community platform, and help nudge people towards more inclusive language in Slack. The most impactful strategy, however, was having the leaders of the community explicitly model these behaviours. People have to see it, believe in it and then become it.

Initially, this was heavily focused on the community leaders, exemplifying the qualities of kindness and generosity and working with folks who might need some support in understanding how these values translated into conduct within our community. While we were still a young community, there were people for whom this was a change from their usual way of engaging with others. Eventually, over time, people started to take this on themselves, and the community really started to become self-moderating to a large extent. When people see and receive kindness and generosity, they tend to respond in kind.

One of the early initiatives that I established to support this culture was sending small tokens of appreciation to those who contributed – a little sticker pack and a thank you note – recognizing their involvement and thanking them for taking the time to contribute to building our community. We also have some unique and highly coveted 'shiny stickers' when people reach certain milestones, which have a handwritten note thanking them for being a part of the community and rejoicing in whatever qualities they demonstrated in their interactions within the community. These gestures, though small and inexpensive, had a significant impact. People absolutely love receiving those little packets of stickers and often share their excitement on social media and comment about how welcomed they feel. I also love writing these hand-written notes!

We tracked these engagements using a Community CRM called Savannah, which helped us understand our community better and identify experts for specific topics. I recommend using a Community CRM to nurture and grow your community effectively. It was one of my earliest learnings, really, that we needed a way to understand our community as we started to scale. The tool also helps us to identify experts who talk a lot about specific topics if we need to find someone to answer a question or be on an advisory group, for example. As the community scaled, I wasn't able to be everywhere and watch every conversation, so this allowed the data to come to me when I needed it.

Listening to our community members was crucial during the growth and scaling phase. At one point, we received complaints from our most active members about repetitive questions being asked in multiple places, particularly in Slack, where people often didn't search for previous answers. This was wasting the valuable time of our contributors and not helping users to find answers efficiently. We decided to direct all support questions to our public forums, setting up nudges to encourage this behaviour. We also enabled features like marking replies as accepted answers, helping future visitors to find resolutions quickly.

Reflecting on our journey, I realize that the initial growth phase was one of the most challenging stages. Establishing a clear culture and engaging members required consistent effort and patience in abundance. With relatively small numbers of people engaging, it felt like talking into an echo chamber at times and being very pedantic, but the efforts really paid off. Seeing the community transform into a self-moderating, supportive space has been incredibly rewarding. If I could do anything differently, I would have focused on defining and communicating our values earlier.

Looking ahead, I feel that we have built some strong foundations upon which our community will continue to grow and thrive. The universal principles of kindness and generosity across cultures, languages and borders. By fostering a culture where everyone feels valued and supported, we can ensure sustainable growth and a positive impact on all members.

Sarah Lewis

Sarah is an award-winning writer and the director of Writers' HQ. She studied creative writing at the University of East Anglia where she won the David Higham Award, and has been mentored by critically acclaimed authors Peter Hobbs and Leone Ross.

Writers' HQ began as a monthly one-day writing retreat in Brighton that I set up to carve time away from my young family to write. I didn't really expect anything to come of it – I literally just hired a room one day and asked on X, formerly known as Twitter, if anyone wanted to join me – and 20 people turned up. So, I started running them monthly and then gradually a small community grew from that and set up some more retreats in different locations, then the online courses evolved and then the online community evolved and now it's something of a behemoth. That makes it sound like it was an easy straight line, but it's very much been a wild ride.

Our tone of voice has been the same from the beginning and it connected with people straight away. It's meant that we've very much gathered our people, which is one of the things that makes the Writers' HQ community special – we're all aligned around a specific idea of writing as something deeply important in ways we perhaps don't quite fully understand. Our courses and events have broadly all run smoothly. A lot of that I think is about a willingness to try stuff and see what works. There are plenty of things we've launched that have faded into obscurity or we've had to stop because they simply didn't work, and that's fine.

Our community was happily trundling along, and we've always had a core of superfans, which is amazing, but it was the pandemic that really exploded our online community. Super early on, as soon as we realized the schools were going to close and that we were going to have to shut down our real-life events, we planned a full programme of free events for the first two or three months of the pandemic, and that made our community explode in size.

The main thing that has not gone well and has consistently not gone well is tech. We have, from the beginning to now, had an absolute nightmare with our website. At first, I built our website, and it was kind of fine. This was over 10 years ago so a lot of out-the-box solutions didn't exist. Then we got targeted by hackers who kept taking the site down, then we had a string of bad external developers. The knock-on effect of that is that previously I haven't been able to spend as much time with people, with the community, as I wanted, because of constant firefighting. A digital community has particular needs – it's not just about putting people in a forum together – and if we're struggling to get the basic underpinning right then those needs aren't being met.

Over the years we've found community moderation to be tricky. Volunteer moderators don't always work out for various reasons, and I never really anticipated such a large community, so I'm still working out how to make it all fit together, what kind of community management we need, how to keep everyone safe and foster an environment where people are liberated to write the stories they need to write.

I also want to say that keeping a community safe is simple; we have absolutely zero tolerance for any kind of intolerance. But there is also complexity, there are always difficult conversations to be had. Especially in an online space where most communication happens in text and misunderstandings are rife. The kind of conversations that come up in our community are things like what stories do we have a right to tell? People feel very strongly about their stories and about Writers' HQ as a space, so things have been known to get heated, but broadly we all look after each other, which is something I value immensely.

Possibly the most unexpected issue was the post-pandemic online drop-off. When people went back to work and were allowed outside again, the online community quietened down and we weren't prepared for that, so there were kind of baggy spaces with not enough people in them.

There's so much I would have done differently.

I would have a clear strategy at the beginning! I would invest more in the community infrastructure from the beginning – the technology that underpins it, and the support and contact people get on the forums.

I still feel firmly in the growth phase. For me right now that's about looking back over the last few years, accepting all the many bits I got wrong, putting solid processes in place, getting a sustainable model in place and getting ready to scale.

Yagmur Simsek

Yagmur Simsek is a seasoned SEO and Content Strategist with over 10 years of experience working with B2B and B2C clients. She is the founder of the Search 'n Stuff community, a networking project designed to connect and empower professionals in the digital marketing space.

Building and growing a community has been quite the journey – full of ups and downs, with plenty of lessons learned along the way. It all started pretty naturally for me. I'd been organizing some networking dinners, and I quickly realized that people really enjoy coming together with others who share similar interests. That got me thinking: what if I could create something bigger? A space or a platform where people could regularly connect, share ideas and feel like they belong.

From the start, I was lucky to have a lot of support from my network. Family, friends, colleagues and contacts were not just attending but also offering feedback and suggestions, which helped shape the community from day one. Listening to them early on was key. Their ideas and insights were valuable in ensuring the community met their needs and expectations. But getting things off the ground wasn't easy, even with all that support. I was juggling a full-time job and two startups, so making the time for it was tough. Plus, the money I could sacrifice was tight. I had to fund those first few meetups out of my own pocket, which wasn't exactly easy, but it was necessary to get things rolling.

As the community started to grow, I didn't just stick with the networking dinners. We began organizing a variety of events to keep things exciting, valuable and fun for everyone involved. We put together meetups featuring panel discussions, quickfire talks and even workshops where people could dive deep into specific topics in entertaining events such as cocktail workshops or networking picnics. These events helped to not only bring more people into the community but also to create more meaningful connections and learning opportunities. And then, of course, we decided to take a giant leap and organize a conference. That has been a massive milestone for us and a real test of everything we have built so far.

But growth brings new challenges. One of the biggest challenges for me has been finding sponsors for our events. For smaller meetups, I could cover costs with ticket sales and a bit of my own money, but when we decided to put on our first big conference, it was a whole different (in other words, stressful) journey. The costs were higher, and getting sponsors was tough, especially since many companies had already allocated their budgets by the time I approached them. This taught me a crucial lesson: timing is everything. I realized that reaching out to potential sponsors and partners needs to happen well in advance.

Another thing that caught me off guard was the realization that our website wasn't ready for the scale we were aiming for. I had to build something from scratch that could handle everything we needed, from ticket sales to promotion. This was a big wake-up call about the importance of having your infrastructure in place before you start trying to scale up.

In addition, managing the day-to-day tasks of running and growing the community was more than I could handle on my own. There were so many things to keep on top of – social media, organizing events, sending out pre-event and post-event emails, and just generally keeping the community engaged. Looking back, I wish I'd brought in help sooner. It took me a while to realize that hiring freelancers to help with things would have made a big difference. If I'd done that earlier, we could have grown faster and more smoothly, with more time to focus on big-picture strategies instead of getting stuck in the details.

While scaling the community, time management became a real challenge. It was hard to dedicate the time the community needed to really thrive. But as the community grew, so did the team, and that made a huge difference. Learning to delegate and trust others with responsibilities allowed me to focus on the long-term vision and goals rather than just keeping up with the day-to-day grind. I won't lie. This is still in progress.

One of the most important lessons I learned was the value of sustainable growth. It's tempting to try to expand quickly, but I found that it's better to grow steadily, ensuring you have the right resources and people before taking the next big step. If I could do it all over again, I'd focus more on collaboration from the start. Bringing in help early on would have sped things up and allowed us to reach more people and potential partners. Also, having a solid infrastructure would have saved us a lot of headaches.

In the end, building a community is a journey. It's not a straight path and has its challenges, but it's also incredibly rewarding. Looking back, these experiences have shaped not just the community but also how I approach leadership and collaboration in general, and they are still teaching me a lot of things. I've learned that community building has to come from the heart. The passion and genuine care for the people involved keep the momentum going, even when things get tough. Without that heartfelt connection, it's hard to sustain the energy needed to keep a community alive.

Key takeaways

The experiences shared by our 14 community leaders offer a wealth of insights into their journey of launching, growing and scaling a community. Their stories showcase the diverse strategies they adopted along the way, and, at the same time, the similar themes shared across their challenges.

Many touched on the importance of having a proper infrastructure in place, one that can be leaned back on when addressing problems, and a focus on clearly communicating your code of conduct with your members, which needs to be modelled by those running the community. Several leaders highlighted the impact they saw in connecting members through online and offline events and finding the right balance for one's community.

Key lessons were shared on the importance of prioritizing the needs of your community members and ensuring that their feedback is heard, with a focus on driving engagement and facilitating conversations and connections.

In the next few pages, I invite you to join me in concluding our book together, and I'll share a few additional resources to help inspire you even further in your community building journey.

Conclusion

When I first started writing this book, I approached it with the mind-set of sharing as much as I could from my own knowledge and experience on all things community building.

Having spent the past five years building and growing my own community, Women in Tech SEO (WTS), I wanted to write the book I wish I'd read in my early days.

But I quickly came to the realization that it can't only be based on what I know, because in all honesty, there's a lot I don't know, and I don't have all the answers. There's a lot that I'm still figuring out myself along the way. So, to make it as comprehensive as possible, I needed to ensure it was reflective of what others know as well.

In turn, writing this book became a learning experience for me. I'm so grateful for all the community leaders who shared their knowledge with me in this book.

In launching your community, we discovered that community is, at its heart, about relationships. We saw the importance of having a clearly defined vision and mission and we looked at how important it is to build structure and functionality with your audience in mind and ensure the platform you use meets your community needs.

In growing your community, we talked about the value of focusing on quality over quantity and building meaningful interactions. We discussed strategies for retaining members and prepared for challenges that might come our way.

In scaling your community, we examined how to capture and action community insights, how to develop partnerships and the value these can provide to your business. Finally, we looked at building for the future, focusing on sustainability and putting together a long-term plan.

Throughout the book, we heard from community-first brands and leaders to help us learn and understand how we can put all this into practice.

If there is only one thing you take away from this book, it would be to go back to what we said at the very start: Find your why.

Make sure you know and believe in the why behind your community. Clearly define your why and hold it up against every community decision you make.

And remember: there is no community without its members. Prioritize your members in all your decisions, onboard them, engage them, listen to them, involve them and communicate with them every step of the way. Your members are rooting for you, brainstorming with you, helping you uncover ideas and opportunities, and willing you to succeed.

I truly believe the future of marketing *is* community.

Community goes far beyond brand awareness or engagement – it's the next level of retention and loyalty. Community is unique in every shape and form, and it simply can't be replicated. But that makes it a long-term game, it doesn't happen overnight – and you need to be prepared to invest in it, to see the outcome.

If you made it this far, thank YOU.

Thank you for joining me on this journey; I hope it was refreshing, inspiring and exactly what you were looking for to help you and your community thrive.

Further resources

Here are a few resources and communities to help inspire you further during your community building journey.

Books

If you're looking for more books to read on community marketing, here are the three books I read myself before writing my own book:

- **Build your community** by Richard Millington
- **Community is your currency** by Daisy Morris
- **Belonging to the brand** by Mark Schaefer

Websites

Here are two websites full of resources that I regularly referred to throughout the book:

- **Feverbee.com:** A wealth of community building resources, case studies and insights
- **Steadfastcollective.com:** The team behind the Digital Community Leaders Report

Communities

Here are communities that I love and that inspire me every day to become a better community leader:

- **Women in Tech SEO (WTS):** Of course, I have to put my community at the top, but genuinely, this is where I met some of the best people in my professional career, a community for all people of marginalized genders in the SEO and marketing space

- **The Digital Marketing Union (DMU):** An online membership community of independent marketers
- **The Freelance Coalition for Developing Countries (FCDC):** A nonprofit organization for BIPOC freelancers in the marketing industry
- **The Sp_ce:** From the team behind Watch This Sp_ce, this is a community of people committed to driving diversity and inclusion in their workplaces
- **Coding Black Females:** A nonprofit organization that provides opportunities for Black female developers
- **Love Her Wild:** A nonprofit adventure community for women, providing opportunities, support and funding to make the outdoors more accessible
- **Next Tech Girls:** A community focused on inspiring today's girls in education to become tomorrow's women in technology
- **The 93% Club:** A members' club for people who went to state schools with the mission to dismantle class inequality through the power of community
- **Writers' HQ:** A community for writers that runs affordable creative writing courses, retreats and workshops

INDEX

Looking for another book?

Explore our award-winning
books from global business
experts in Marketing and Sales

Scan the code to browse

www.koganpage.com/marketing

More from Kogan Page

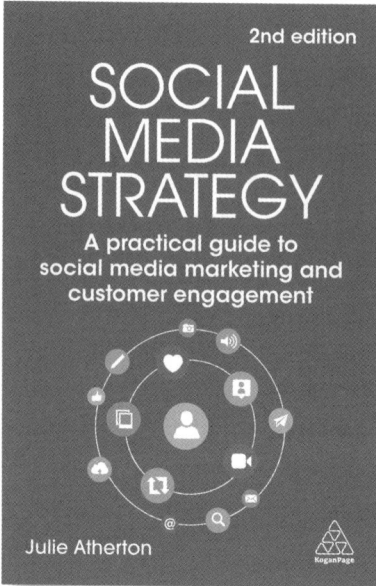

2nd edition

SOCIAL MEDIA STRATEGY

A practical guide to social media marketing and customer engagement

Julie Atherton

ISBN: 9781398609990

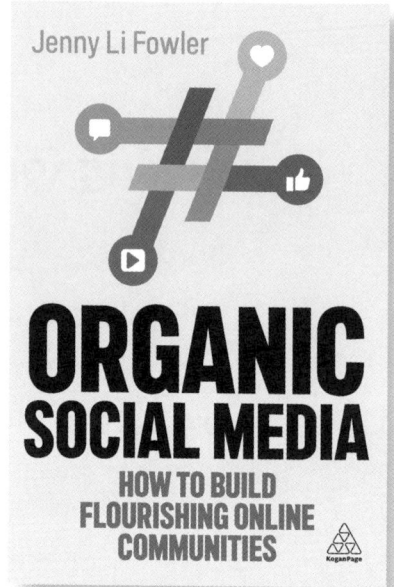

Jenny Li Fowler

ORGANIC SOCIAL MEDIA

HOW TO BUILD FLOURISHING ONLINE COMMUNITIES

ISBN: 9781398612976

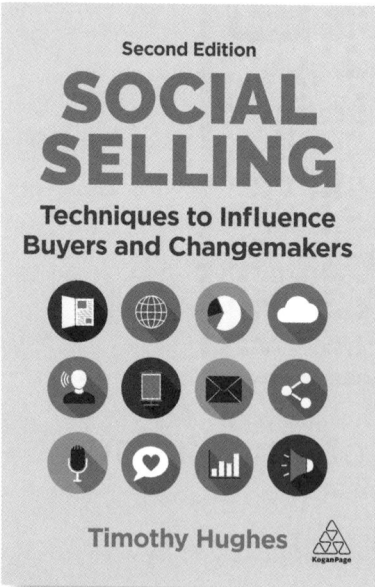

Second Edition

SOCIAL SELLING

Techniques to Influence Buyers and Changemakers

Timothy Hughes

ISBN: 9781398607323

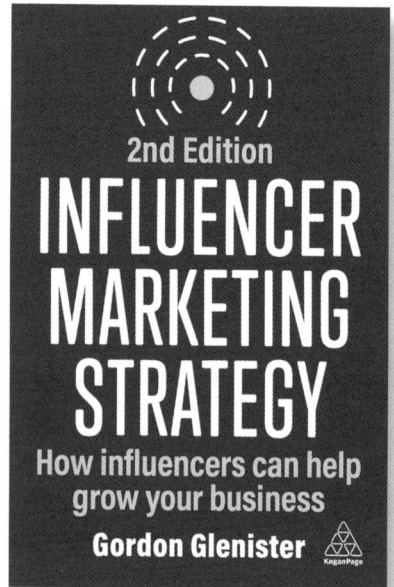

2nd Edition

INFLUENCER MARKETING STRATEGY

How influencers can help grow your business

Gordon Glenister

ISBN: 9781398615236

www.koganpage.com